Henry Corbet

Tales and Traits of Sporting Life

Henry Corbet

Tales and Traits of Sporting Life

ISBN/EAN: 9783742899224

Manufactured in Europe, USA, Canada, Australia, Japa

Cover: Foto ©Thomas Meinert / pixelio.de

Manufactured and distributed by brebook publishing software (www.brebook.com)

Henry Corbet

Tales and Traits of Sporting Life

TALES AND TRAITS

OF

SPORTING LIFE.

BY

HENRY CORBET.

LONDON:
ROGERSON AND TUXFORD, 246, STRAND.

1864.

CONTENTS.

THE PROFIT AND LOSS	Page 1
THE THISTLE DOWN	13
JOHN GULLY	26
THE FARMER'S STORY	34
MODERN HUNTING SONG	44
THE HARD-UP	46
OLD JOHN DAY	55
THE PRIVATE PUPIL	68
THE FATE OF ACTÆON	76
A COPER'S CONFESSION	87
FULWAR CRAVEN—"A BIT OF A CHARACTER"	99
THE GREAT HANDICAP RACE	109
GOODWOOD IN THE DAYS OF THE LATE DUKE	116
THE BANISHED MAID	125
A DECEIVING HORSE	128
THE GREAT HORSE AND HOUND SHOW	133
A SECOND FOX	150
A DESPERATE MAN	155
THE LOVE BIRD	162
THE BELLES OF SWINDON	167
THE FAVOURITE	170
THE LAST OF THE CHIFNEYS	176
THE BREEDING OF HUNTERS AND HACKS	183

TALES AND TRAITS

OF

SPORTING LIFE.

THE PROFIT AND LOSS.

A MAN that's born and bred a sportsman can't help feeling proud of it. I should think it was so all the world over, as I am sure it is here. A man that has "a propensity" must show, and suffer for, it sooner or later. I should think it was so with all, as I am too sure it has been with me. At school it came out, as the M. D.s say, pretty kind on me. Derby winners all off by heart, foxes' brushes always to be found in the play-box, and a tolerably good recollection of last Christmas' equestrian performances, brought me a proper share of reverence that a change in the sovereignty of the County Hounds did everything to establish. A new Master for the hounds brought a new boy for the Doctor. The new boy's father was a friend of my father; and the next Saint's Day saw a pair of us off for the kennels, big in white cords and cover hacks. That did it outright; *his* father kept hounds, *my* father kept race-horses; and certainly if ever the proper qualification for a sportsman brought becoming dignity with it, here we enjoyed it in full force. Everybody

B

bowed down before it; fellows whose mothers and sisters went to Court every time the Court went itself; long-pedigreed gentlemen with uncles in " the Lords;" young Pluti, with family fortunes in the Indies—all alike sung small before our rather overdone terms and technicalities. The very masters occasionally " opened" on it; and the action of *quadrupedante putrem,* the force of *sunt quos curriculo,* or anything of that sort, generally ended in coming to us for an authority or an example. We had all the pride of the sportsman here, and, upon my life! I really believe, without ever having once suffered for the propensity.

My " hobbydyhoyish" days followed suit about as naturally as could be expected. For *fidus Achates* I won't answer, as he started to stifle his early impressions amongst the Rajahs and tigers. For self, however, the fates were propitious. At nineteen, I subscribed to the " Calendar," and studied the " Stud Book." At two-and-twenty, I could handicap horses—aye, and weigh them well too. The propensity began to develop itself in earnest; and as fast and firm as ever came the love of " a bit of coaching " across some of us, came the desire for " a bit of plating " on me.

" Nice, quiet, clean little place this, waiter—market-town, too—isn't it?"

" Oh! dear, yes, sir; corn and cattle market every Saturday, and butter and egg market every Wednesday as well."

" Ah! indeed; and any sport too?"

" Beg pardon, sir,—any what?"

" Any sport—any racing?"

" Racing, sir! Races every autumn; two days, sir; balls and ordinaries held at this house, sir; very capital sport indeed, I'm told, sir. Got the bill in the bar, sir; perhaps you'd like to see it?"

And away goes the waiter, and back he comes again with what he calls "the bill of sport" in one hand, and the Tally-ho sauce in the other. Shows what it is to be a sportsman; how the pride will out, and the propensity—as a bill of another sort will no doubt tell us to-morrow morning—suffer for it. Sportsmen hold a very high, liberal kind of character; and landlords always do their part to make them work up to it.

But to get back to my individual propensity—the bit of plating—the start for which was hardly as good as I had counted on. Two legs—or rather, to be correct, as he'd only three when we "claimed" him—a leg and a half on the sly in a hurdle jumper was the way it broke out. "To pay half the expenses and have half the profits"—with that most sagacious insertion "*if any*"—was the agreement; to pay all the expenses, and have no profits, more like my actual part in it. The Co. in the concern, who managed, trained, and rode "Daring Ranger" himself, had got a name for doing things rather close; a vulgar notion which our "account," I must say, did much to belie. Everything, from weights and scales, to boots and chambermaid, had been done *en prince*. So astounding, indeed, sounded the sum total, that when my friend, in something like a fit of offended dignity, offered to take my share of the nag for my share of the bill, I jumped at once at the exchange, and let him in, in a moment, as "sole proprietor." Of course the only plan for bettering this was to stop up the propensity altogether, or to have a plater all to myself; and of course everybody can give a tolerably good guess as to which of the two events was the more likely to come off first. From a very worthy man—a public trainer, who lived in the neighbourhood, I learnt that nothing was so likely to answer as a little racing in a quiet way, in support of which opinion he called my attention to the case of one Captain Sullivan. The Captain, a patron of a little racing in a quiet way, and my Mentor's establishment in particular, followed it up till it followed him to Dover; and then the same paper which announced his departure for the continent, also contained an intimation to this effect—that if a certain Captain S. did not take away his mare "the Mountain Maid," and pay her expenses at the same time, she would be sold forthwith to pay them. Considering how many there would have been too happy to take the Captain himself, it was by no means extraordinary to find he paid no attention to this piece of courtesy, and as he didn't, I did the expenses. Changing her colours, but not her quarters, the Mountain Maid commenced her fourth year and second season in my name.

And an exciting season we had of it, too! The way Sam Mane used to sit down and grind his teeth at my poor filly was something awful to see, and the heart with which she continued to answer him, something wondrous to look upon. "Game little animal that, sir, as ever was stripped;" and so she was certainly if you came to *that;* but that wasn't all. Second, second, and second, without end; nothing better, or as some knowing gentleman affirmed, nothing worse. Had there ever been such a thing in classic story as a female Tantalus, I should certainly have insulted the Captain by changing her name; but as I believe there is not, on we went, day after day, and week after week, running for every heat and everything. The round of rather shy meetings we visited that summer, had they possessed one grain of gratitude, would have clubbed up for a handsome testimonial in return for the vast addition to their sport our presence had occasioned. As it really happened, however, they did'nt; and so, with a very spotless, profitless, maiden reputation, we wound up the year with one try more close home. Here, *mirabile dictu*, amidst the shouts of our friends and relations, and the very audible hisses of Mr. Mane, the Mountain Maid did manage to win—a heat—the first heat—and to spring a sinew—a back sinew—in the second. Having achieved this agreeable surprise she hobbled back to nurse, leaving her "worthy owner," as they called him at dinner, with some fearful forebodings touching those travelling expenses he had already had a taste of. "Entry here—" "stake there—" "paid to jockey,"&c. &c., with all the entertaining sundries of "self and lad," over and over again. If they have only had the taste too to do it *en prince*, the propensity to suffer for will become "all his own" with a vengeance!

The fortunes of this day, though, didn't end here, for I had found out another propensity quite as difficult to conquer as even a bit of plating. I was hit hard again; aye, and by a pair of black eyes that I had passed over a hundred and fifty times before. But then, "the sweet sympathy" is the very secret of love after all; and to meet those sparklers all sparkle as the Mountain Maid ran home something like a clever winner in number one, and to mark them shaded over as she crept in something like a break-down in number two, was more than enough for me. They were so glad, and then so sorry; the gratulation and consolation followed so fervidly, I couldn't but feel it; and opportunity came so aptly, I couldn't but follow up what I felt. My racing was over, for that year at any rate; and it would be still some time yet ere my half-hack, half-hunter, came into the more worthy half of his work; nothing for it, then, but to indulge the propensity, and so away we went according-*ly*. A fairer match-maker, I will say, never was needed; and by the first Monday in November, as they date it at Melton, I fancied we were getting to something like terms.

"Do you like butter'd toast?"

"Yes."

"Butter'd on both sides?"

"Yes."

"Will you marry me?"

And here, according to all the rules of common delicacy, our sweet sympathy came to a bit of a check, which was still got tolerably well over with an appeal that must be made to "my aunt." This, though, was more than I'd prepared for; and good-collar'd one, as I flattered myself to be, I confess I couln't "come again" so early as that; so the end of it was that Emmy must ask herself. Now the idea of a man to a maiden aunt is always dreadful enough anyhow; but when that man came to be singled out as myself, it was all U. P. in a minute.

"No, my dear girl—no! If you have any regard for my good opinion—(*i.e.* any hopes of the little Pontybwnbyllyn estate)—I am sure you'll think no more of him. No chance of happiness to be had with such a husband as that."

Hearing this wholesale condemnation, Emily naturally began to whimper a little, and to "know the reason why?"

"William's very steady, aunt: he doesn't drink, you know?"

"No—not yet, perhaps; that's a vice that's more common after than before marriage: but it isn't that."

"And he goes to church every Sunday morning."

"Oh! yes, miss; I can see people in church as well as you, I hope; though, perhaps, without looking so constantly at them. It isn't that."

"And he doesn't swear, dear aunt."

"No; I really trust he does not dis———"

"Except, to be sure, when he was very violent in his protestations to me, and that———"

"Thank Heaven, I know nothing at all about."

And then came the cigars, and as it "wasn't that" either—not his drinking, smoking, swearing, nor church-going—Emmy became a little more confident, offered to "give it up," and at length, pressing the old lady rather closely, got out the grand secret in these words:—

"*He keeps a race-horse,*" Miss Emma; and in my opinion a man that keeps a race-horse will very soon find he can't keep a wife."

That was a stopper certainly; and the old woman gave it out as if she thought so too. If I'd been ruined by railroads, or found guilty of forgery, there might have been hopes; but "he keeps a race-horse" was too much. Poor Emmy shut up shop in half a second, and was as jealous as possible of our mutual acquaintance, the Mountain Maid, the next time she saw me. Evidently it was a "to be or not to be;" and "deeply engaged" as I was, and somewhat staggered with our summer's run, of second-rate success, no wonder I soon struck under. The marrying man against the racing man—"heads!" for the turf, and down it came for matrimony in the shape of a woman. A breeder of the forbidden fruit, as if to support me in my good resolution, very politely became "deceased" just at the time, and into his catalogue went "my first love." At the end of the year, with a staring coat and a bandaged leg, she was put up, and knocked down for fifty minus what I had originally paid over for her on the gallant Captain's account. No matter, I was married, and one propensity had to suffer for the other.

* * * * * *

Whether 'twas the want of a race-horse or not, I won't pretend to say; but certainly, somehow or other, I seemed to run on pretty well as a Benedick. Drank a little, smoked a little, went to church a little, and got the credit for certain other small virtues of the same kind. So well, indeed, did I behave, that, as if in return for the couple of ponies I had sacrificed at the sale, aunty stood "Sam" for a pair of Galloways—fourteen hands, even steppers, swish tales, small heads, and all "commy fow." These went a great way towards pleasing everybody; made my half-hunter a whole one outright, and gave the ladies a taste for horse-flesh I hoped might improve. And so it did, for when the autumn came again, and the races came again, they volunteered at once for a drive to the course, and so of course to the course we went. There's a very fine line to draw with the world between going to a race and keeping a race-horse—

"I thought so once, but now I know it."

"Well, how d'ye do? What's to win the Handicap?" Third race on the card, and *the* race of the day. Two Newmarketers, an elegant extract from Epsom, another from Danebury, and, strange enough, my old venture, the Mountain Maid (now the property of a Mr. John Jones), going for it. Even on Newmarket; three to one against John Day, and anything you like to ask from a pound of *Goold* to a pewter-pot about the plater.

She's well in too—5 yrs. 7st. 1lb., and just her distance —two miles and a half—shouldn't wonder to see her wear 'em out now, if the leg don't give. And Sam Mane again, in the old pink and white jacket, going to ride her!

"How d'ye do, Mr. Mane?"

"How do *you* do, sir? Hope I see you well."

"Pretty well, thank you. So you're going to make play with the old mare, I hear?"

"Why, yes, sir; keep her in front as long as we can."

And keep her in front he did. First time passed the stand with a clear lead, and going well within herself.

"Ah! she'll come back to 'em by next time," sneered the even bettors.

But she didn't, though. "Never reached her at all, sir." Won in a canter by three lengths, and the third beaten half a distance!

"Tally-ho!" roared the second Steward as he galloped by our station. "Tally-ho!" echoed somebody else, quite as loud, though he wasn't a Steward at all; and then commenced "a scene" round my little carriage, which the Derby homeward reporters would phrase as one "that beggars description." For the first few seconds or so, I felt much inclined to play Ducrow on the backs of the ponies—*why*, I'm sure I can't say. Then I snapt the crop of my whip in endeavouring to send it safe home—*how*, I'm sure I don't know; and then up rolled Primeport, the wine merchant, with a couple of champagne bottles in one hand, half-a-dozen glasses neck-and-neck in the other, and the cork-screw between his teeth.

"Wish you joy, old fellow—can't shake hands with you just yet, though. How d'ye do, ladies? This *is* pleasant, isn't it? Happy as queens, I can see."

And after him, over the ropes, came young Broughton, the doctor, and nearly over the heads of the ponies as well. " Took twenty to one to a fiver about her three minutes before starting—won a hundred clear. Ah ! Miss MacRichards, lucky dog, isn't he ? Won't abuse the race-horses now—eh, ladies ?"

But " the ladies " were evidently nonplussed, and their conductor somewhat confused. What could it all be to them ?

" Who is he ?" inquired my wife ; " point him out to us."

"Yes, *do* show us this fortunate Mr. Jones," joined in Miss MacRichards.

" Show you who ?" said Primeport, who was grinding away at a bottle between his knees. " Show you this Mr. Jones. Yes, that I will in a twinkling. Here he stands as large as life, and twice as happy, the husband of that sweet lady, and the real owner of the Mountain 'Maid. Had her on the quiet, you see, all through, and now she's gained him two hundred and twenty-five pounds at one start. Prove it in a minute. Fifteen small forfeits—five times five, seventy-five—then two at fifteen each, that's thirty more, a hundred and five—and fifty ad——"

But just here the enthusiastic ready-reckoner stopped short : there was something going on, he, for one, never bargained for. Miss Mac. had become a body of ice, quite as quick as ever Mrs. Lot took to the pillar of salt ; and my little woman certainly evinced every disposition, as the actors say, to play up to her. Secrets are quite a toss-up in women's hands, and it is all an open question how they will tell, let the premises be ever so promising. In this instance the effect was never for a moment in doubt. Prime had committed himself, and condemned me ; and when our trusty pilot, Mr. Mane, strolled up for a glass of champagne, I could plainly see, from *his* countenance, that he was reading in mine a clear case of having " taken* a liberty " with my own mare. Put him right I could not; and so, after agreeing to another taste of the champagne, which, for want of customers, poor Prime was turning to home consumption, the silk-shirted hero made again for the weighing-house, with the point of his whip in his mouth, and evidently deeply engaged in an inward argument, as to his pink-and-white patron being more rogue or fool.

I was thinking of something the same sort myself.

To him succeeded our Tally-ho friend, all on the lookout, with the word in his mouth, and the book in his hand. " Come now, then, Fortunatus, how many subscriptions am I to put you down for?"

" Well, I think one must——"

" *One!* you avaricious rascal!—*one!* after sweeping off that pocketful of money! Come, come, our fair friends here, I know, will make him behave better than that. Let's see—'what's your d——d name?' as the man in the play says. Ah! William Alphonzo Oxford, Esq. *Ditto ditto* to that; and then, of course, *Mrs.* William Alphonzo Oxford, Esq. Miss Richards, I'm sure you'll let me chronicle you in such good company?"

" Not at present, sir,—that is, if I am permitted to say no," replied that amiable lady, with a frosty-faced smile that passed the gentlemen tout on in less than no time.

Matters were getting serious indeed, and as a *sequitur*, some of the scamps began to laugh; but, egad! 'twas no laughing matter either. Pontybwnbyllyn never looked

---

"Taking a liberty" with a horse stands for laying long odds against him.

worse; and I couldn't help saying to myself, " All this is capital hedging for a certain dear cousin of ours thrice removed." To be sure he'd been through every step of the Rake's Progress, from strolling playing to methodist preaching, and was now existing in Calais on hopes and *post obits;* but, with all his faults, he had never had a race-horse, and ——

" Might I trouble you, Mr. Oxford, to put me down at my little cottage, as I fear I shall be quite out of place at your rejoicings this evening? In fact, to tell you the truth, I can't help thinking that at the best THE PROFIT AND LOSS in this racing are strangely conflicting."

And again I was thinking of something the same sort myself.

Something must be done, and if 'twere done at all, 'twere better it were done quickly. That something, as it generally does, meant one thing. The hammer must a second time relieve me, and the Hyde Park Corner corner of the *Morning Post* speak for itself:—" On Monday next, without reserve, the property of a gentleman, the Mountain Maid, five years old, winner of the South Western Handicap, by Muley Moloch, out of the Maid of Llangollen, by Langar."

She's gone!—for a hundred and ten more, though, than the Captain was credited for; and like him, I am happy to say, out of the country. A Mr. Johannisbergh, or Brœnenberg, or some such name, has escorted her to Prussia, so that I shall never be tempted again. I have got a good precedent too. As did poor Lord George, I have stopped my Calendar, and entered on another propensity. At this writing, I have half-a-dozen dahlias in strong work, and am open at any time to an even fiver that I am first, second, or third for the Amateur's Cup.

THE THISTLE DOWN.

A LONG ten miles at last from all the bustle of the Line, let us stay for a moment on the brow of this next hill, to enjoy in quiet the glorious view that breaks before us. Ridged in on one of the highest ranges of England, what an undulating sweep of soft green sward now meets the eye! There may be some further boundary, but it is all illimitable in the horizon, and the sweet springy down-land flows on in an ocean of unbroken plain. Little care would the husbandman seem to have hereabouts, although in that hollow to the left you note the comfortable well-to-do homestead of Thistley Grove. Yet farther away to the right, buried in the clump of trees from which it takes its title, is Elm Down—the high home of the gaze-hound—famous for the Ladies Sylvia, Aurora, and Diana, who manage their prancing palfreys so gracefully, and talk so learnedly to the admiring crowd of "turn," "wrench," and "go-by." Let your glance rest again under that narrow belt of firs just rising from another dip of the wavy open, and tell us what you see there. Nothing but some sheep? Then the lambs can scarcely keep themselves warm this nipping March morning; for, look again, and there are some half-dozen of them off, as hard as they can go! A capital pace it is, too, for now that orderly methodical line is lost. And the lambs, as they draw towards us, while—somewhat scared—we stand aside to make way for them, gradually develop into a string of long-striding, carefully-clothed horses, snorting in all the glow of speed and health as they rush past, and coping in their strength with the tiny lads who sit them so close and hold them so hard. They are stopping, however, as they reach the rest of the flock again, and the shepherd might, perhaps, be kind enough to let us have a more composed look at them.

Mr. Shepherd, who, in his well-cut jacket and rifleman leggings, might be a sporting farmer or fox-hunter in mufti, will be "only too happy" to show us and tell us all he can. There would really seem to be no secret about it; and were the laird himself down—the owner of these thirty or forty thorough-breds—he would only join our Mentor in calling them over to us. Let us begin with that company of five—the little lot, by-the-by, being worth at the very least some twenty thousand pounds. Mark that lazy, careless, self-satisfied looking "old horse" as they fondly call him, which leads the string! See how the boy has actually to kick him along in his lolloping walk, or even to strike at him sharply through the heavy clothing with his ash plant! But the chesnut, as he honours you with just one sagacious glance through that plaided cowl, says, as plainly as can be, that he knows this is all child's play, and that he can go away when he is really wanted to go. He speaks but the simple truth, for Barnoldby is the champion of his order, the best horse in the world at this moment, who has done more, and has done it better, and has worn longer than anything else we should see, were our pilgrimage on the Thistle Down to reach on to its utmost limit. The Derby, the Royal Cup, the Great Two-year-old—even Mr. Shepherd can scarcely trust his memory to tell of all that low lengthy animal has achieved. So we come on to the next in order to him. "A three-year-old colt, sir, that we call Aristophanes," is the simple introduction, given with an air of indifference, which we attempt so indifferently to echo as to bring up an involuntary smile on the countenance of our guide. And this is Aristophanes! This resolute powerful bay, who follows on with something in his air and manner of indolent hauteur, is the great favourite for the great race of the year. This is the horse that the papers write about, the clubs talk about, and the world perpetually thinks about. Should he be heard to cough, it might make a difference of thousands. Were he to spring a sinew, or throw a curb, or even to turn up that haughty nostril of his over the next feed of corn, the knowledge of such a calamity would convulse the market. There are great men who would give much for the opportunity to see what we shall now, as Mr. Shepherd sends the illustrious five down to the other end of the plantation, with orders to "come along at a pretty good pace."

Now keep your eyes open, as old Barnoldby leads off, almost mechanically, with the lad hustling and threatening, to force him out. But he has done his duty ably enough already, and our gaze centres, some few lengths off, on his successor. Mr. Shepherd can bear it. "The crack" is going sweetly, and the more he extends himself, the more determinedly he pulls at his rider, the more you like him. There is the long, even, stealthy, almost slow-seeming stride, like the steady stroke of the accomplished swimmer; and yet with what liberty he strikes out! how well his hind-legs come under him! and with what courage he faces the hill, as old Barnoldby, having made a pace at last, appears wickedly inclined to find out what the young one can do! Their Two Thousand nag is behind him, a strong favourite for the Spring Handicap fourth, and a lop-eared Colonist of high character last. They are all good; but we linger over Aristophanes as he walks back, only all the better for his breathing, and close at once with the invitation to see him in his box. By the way, though that bevy of bays and greys yonder are the lambkins we first met with; and the handsome aged horse, even with so much substance about him, is still good enough to win Royal Plates, though the laird does talk of riding him in the Park.

But Mr. Shepherd thinks we had better stroll on to the house, that Thistley Grove which looked so comfortable in the distance, and where a biscuit and a glass of Barnoldby sherry await us. The rooks in the long elm avenues are busy in their preparations for a welcome to the little strangers; while the famous dowagers of high descent, and worth at least a thousand pounds each, are looking to maternal cares of their own, as they group themselves under the grand old trunks, or walk off, in some disdain that their dishevelled beauties should be made a mark for the sight-seeing stranger. There are yearlings, already of fabulous prices; an interesting invalid, Sweet Blossom, with a refined melancholy about her that is quite catching: and the prettiest horse in England, who has had the terrible misfortune to " hit his leg," and is in physic as a consequence. That massive door-Belle is a daughter of the rare old Grantley hound, and this shorthorn heifer has a pedigree as long as that of Aristophanes himself, whose toilet by this time must surely be completed. He has been brushed and wisped until his brownish hard-coloured coat shines again; his large flat legs are duly washed and bandaged; his nostrils spunged out; his long thin mane neatly combed and arranged. He is just set fair, in fact, with the hood finally thrown over his quarter-piece, when, to his manifest disgust, we are ushered into his box.

No one likes to be interfered with at dinner-time, and "Harry" strikes out rather angrily with his near fore-leg when his valet proceeds once more to strip him. That eye is full of character, as he turns it upon you, but the long lean head is not so handsome as it is expressive; yet how finely it is set on to his thin somewhat straight neck, and how beautifully that, again, fits into his magnificent sloping shoulders! There is breadth and freedom of play, supported by long powerful arms and short wiry legs, heavier in the bone than any hairy-heeled John Jolly that ever drew a drayman. Come a little more forward, and glance over that strong muscular back, those drooping quarters, and big clean hocks—and then say if the thorough-bred horse, in high condition, be not a very hero of strength and swiftness! He would gallop the far-famed Arabian of the desert to death, and you would be but as an infant with him. He would rush off with you in his first canter, docile and sluggish as he was at exercise; and with one lash out of that handsome haunch he would send you far over his head; or "order" you out of his box in an instant, as you awkwardly attempt to "go up to" him. Somewhat grim is the humour of Aristophanes; and, as we hear as plainly as he does the rattle of his dinner-service, suppose we wish him good morning, and assure Mr. Shepherd confidentially, when once more in the open, that he is the very finest Derby horse we ever saw, and that we shall seriously think about backing him for a "stoater," "a monkey," "a hyæna," or—a two-shilling piece.

There are nearly forty others to strip and talk over,

many of established repute, more of coming promise, and all, save the handsome Park horse that is to be, of the highest and purest lineage. And now that we have seen them, and when we begin to tire of studying so perfect a picture, let us pause for a minute, to reflect over its peculiar tone and treatment, and to ask were you ever over any manufactory—did you ever inspect any gigantic "establishment," where the good genius of rule and order had a better home than at Thistley? Have you found a stirrup-leather out of place? Have you noticed the tiniest of those little lads ever flurried or awkward over his work? Have you heard an oath, or so much as an angry word, since we have been here? "Don't speak so sharply to your mare, boy!" was Mr. Shepherd's mild reproof to the lad who cried out at the white-legged filly when she twisted round suddenly on her way home; and again: "I say, young gentleman, would'nt you look all the better if you had your hair cut?" to another, much rejoicing in his golden locks. But we will have a word ourselves with a third—this natty youth coming across the yard, with his horse's muzzle packed, as some travellers will their sponge-bags, with all kinds of toilet-traps. Jack Horner is his name, and he was born in London; but he came down to Mr. Shepherd as an apprentice, some three years since. He looks about twelve years of age, but rather indignantly says he is past fifteen, and that he does not weigh four stone. *There* is a combination of fortune's and nature's favours, rarely to be met with in this world! Can any one by any possibility imagine anything more acutely wide-awake than a boy born in London and educated in a racing-stable! who is unnaturally small for his years, who can sit close, hold his own tongue, and the hardest puller in the stable? Go on and prosper, little

Jack Horner! And when the days of thy serving-time are over, you shall jump into a living worth double that of the parson of the parish, and end by having a heavier income-tax than the most famous Q.C. who ever worried a witness or bullied a judge. The nobles of the land shall send in their special retainers, humbly asking that you will appear for them when you can. The anxious telegram shall seek you out. The best of champagne and the oldest of Havannahs shall court your taste; and when you go a courting on your own account, you shall woo the dark-eyed daughter of The Blue Dragon, with armlets of emeralds and pearls of price! "Ah, all very fine, sir," says little Jack Horner—though not without a notion that it may be all very true, with time and luck to help him. At present Jack gets ten pounds a year and a suit of clothes, with three good meals a day, and, despite his weight, a fair share of beef and beer. His one great mission is to look after his horse, for he is rarely called upon to do more. In the summer he is with him by daybreak, if he do not sleep at his heels, in a couch that looks like a corn-bin, but which, with no "double debt to pay," unrols into a bed and nothing more. The attendant sprite of Aristophanes sleeps over him; for that great horse might contrive to cast himself in his box, or the bad fairy might try to come in through the keyhole, or something or other might occur that would need the ready assistance of his body-guard. Dressing his horse lightly over, and feeding him, are amongst the first of Jack Horner's duties, to be followed immediately by the walking exercise—the way on to the Down, the gentle canter, the smart gallop, or the long four-miler that has now generally superseded "the sweat." Horses are no longer loaded with clothes and fagged and scraped, but they get the same amount of work without the unnecessary severity once so general and fatal. Common sense has of late years driven out much of the conventional practice of the training-stable, and a horse is now treated in accordance with his peculiar temper and constitution. Some horses are so nervous that they begin to fidget at the mere sight of the muzzle with which a horse was, as a rule, "set" the night before he ran; and now, not one horse in fifty is ever "set" at all. Others know as readily the intention with which their manes are plaited into thick, heavy tresses—a part of the etiquette costume of the course now by no means so carefully observed as of yore—and some begin to "funk," as the schoolboys say, so soon as the stranger Vulcan comes to shift their light shoes for the still lighter "plates." Certain horses will almost train themselves, without needing any clothing whatever, while grosser animals require continual work. The late Lord Eglinton's famous Van Tromp was a very indolent horse, and took an immense "preparation," two or three good nags being solely employed to lead him in his gallops; while his temper was so bad, that for the last year he was ridden in a muzzle, to prevent his flying at the other horses out. His yet more renowned half-brother, The Flying Dutchman, went, on the contrary, so freely, and pulled so much, that he never had half the work of the other, and usually galloped by himself. But he was of a most excitable temperament, both in and out of the stable.

This great business of galloping over, Jack Horner brings his horse back in his own proper place in the string to the stable, where he is dressed again far more elaborately, and, when "set fair," is fed. A horse in work will eat in a day his six "quarterns" of corn (of sixteen quarterns to the bushel), often mixed with a few old beans, and occasionally, as at Thistley Grove, with some sliced carrots ; while he has hay " at discretion," regulated either by his own delicate appetite, or meted out to his too eager voracity. Then, with the horse left in quiet to his meal, the boy begins to think of his own, which in the summer is breakfast, and in the winter dinner. We may be satisfied that, unless Jack is to have a mount in the next Handicap, there is no use for the muzzle here either; and Mrs. Shepherd has a boy all the way from the North Riding, whose prowess over suet pudding is something marvellous to witness. Almost all the lads are from a distance, for the cottager's wife cannot reconcile it to herself to see her dear Billy crying to come home again; and so surely as he begins to cry, so surely does he go home. Mrs. Shepherd, however, is a good mother to those who stay with her. They go to the village church regularly every Sunday, and there is a chapel-room at the Grove, which is a school-room every evening in the week, and a place of worship on the Sabbath.

On the other side of the Thistle Down, four of Mr. Dominie the public trainer's lads wear surplices as singers in the church of one of the strictest clergymen in Downshire. They attend an evening-school, where the trainer's son is a teacher, and Dominie himself is churchwarden. Had Holcroft lived in these days, he would never have longed for life in London; and *That's your sort!* would have been an echo rather of the green sward than of the green room. Mr. Dominie makes it a condition when hiring a lad that he shall regularly attend a place of worship, and some trainers walk in procession to church with their boys, precisely as if the establishment were an academy where the neighbouring youth were "genteelly boarded." The economy of a public stable is very similar to that of Mr. Shepherd's. The lads get about the same wages, but seldom with the addition of the suit of clothes; and some, but not so many as their employers could wish, are bound apprentice for four or five years on first entering. A really clever child, when so articled, may be turned to considerable profit, for there is a continual demand for such light weights, and of course the master can generally make his own terms as to how they shall share the fees received for riding races for other people. To "*hold his tongue,*" and "*keep his hands down*" are the two golden rules of a jockey boy's life, and the height of his ambition to ride in public. Should he be very successful at first, he is apt to lose his head; and here the indentures do him good service by keeping him in proper control until he has completed his education. Should he then have outgrown the stable in size and weight, he is still qualified to make the best of grooms. To tend on the high-bred horse that is, and not to look after a horse and chaise, clean knives and shoes, dig in the garden, wait at table, and help Mary Anne in her airings with the double-bodied perambulator. Jack Horner's early career has scarcely fitted him for "a place" like this; but if you really have need of a *groom*, the training-stable is as the University for turning out a first-class man. Of late years, private establishments have been coming more and more into fashion, and for a gentleman with anything like a stud of his own, there can be no other so satisfactory or legitimate a means of engaging in the sport. Thistley Grove is at this time about the most successful of any stable in the kingdom, either public or private; and a brother of our Mr. Shepherd was lately in receipt of the highest salary ever paid to a private trainer. He had six hundred pounds a year, with a capital house to live in, and, even beyond this, "farmed" the horses and boys for his employer at so much a head. This scale, however, is considerably beyond the average. As a rule, a trainer is now a well-conducted, comparatively well-educated man, with, of course, the occasional exception we find in every other rank and calling. But the ignorant cunning sot, once too true a type of his order, is dying out with the old-fashioned huntsman, who got drunk as a duty when he had killed his fox.

Let us suppose that the laird of the Thistle Down, in the pride of his heart, has presented you with one of those famous mares we disturbed but now under the elms— more fatal gift, may be, than that Trojan horse whereof old Homer sung in fine, full flowing hexameter. The Dowager Duchess is your own, and straightway your ambition is fired to win the Derby. With good fortune, the year's keep of the mare and other preliminary expenses, your foal has cost you some seventy pounds by the day he is born. Subsequently when weaned, there will be a year and a-half of the idleness of infancy, what time he is being fed with corn, fondled and handled and half broken; and this will call for a full eighty pounds more. Then, in the September previous to entering on his second year, he goes up to school, where he gets board, lodging, attendance, and teaching for somewhere about 50s. a week. The customary charge in a high-class public stable is two guineas a week, including the lad; while to this must be added the smith, saddler, physic, and other incidental charges, to bring up the total. A year and a-half spent thus with Mr. Dominie will add another item to the account of one hundred and ninety pounds; and as you keep him specially to win the Derby, his expenses to and at Epsom will be but some eight pounds more. The stake is one of fifty pounds each, the jockey's fee for a "chance" mount is three pounds—he will expect five hundred if he should win—and so by the time that lilac body and red sleeves is "coloured" on the card —by the time that those three-and-thirty thorough-bred colts have dipped down from the paddock to the post, there is not one amongst them who faces the flag but has cost some four hundred pounds to get there. During the year 1861, between eighteen and nineteen hundred horses actually ran in England and Ireland, while there were many others which, from a variety of circumstances, never appeared, although in training. Beyond these, even, we must include the steeple-chasers, whose names rarely appear in the strictly legitimate records of Weatherby. And we may thus guess at the amount of money expended on horse-flesh, living at the rate of from two pounds five shillings to two pounds ten shillings a week each horse. The large breeding establishments, the outrageously heavy travelling expenses, when a horse pays a guinea a night for his box, and other items of outlay, we must not stay to consider, but "keeping" them to their work when at home, they have, of course, the very best of oats and hay, all bought in at the best prices; while a trainer will often pay a farmer more for the privilege to exercise on a down, than the tenant gives for it as a sheep-walk. So far from this being a detriment to the land, "the bite" is nowhere so sweet as where the horses gallop; and the flock will continue to follow the string, as they change from one side of the hill to the other.

Let us leave the high-mettled where we first found him, in such good companionship, with the little lambs

mocking his long stride, as they run matches against each
other to the tinkling of the starting-bell with which the
wandering ewe will clear the way. How different in its
sober, monotonous echo, to that quick, thrilling alarum
which proclaims "*they're off!*" When, in the noise and
turmoil of the crowded course, we are challenged on every
side by the hoarse husky Ishmaelite who will "lay agen"
everything and everybody—when, amidst the din of dis-
cord and the wild revelry of such a holiday, we catch a
glimpse of the yellow jacket of Aristophanes as he sweeps
by in his canter, or struggles home to a chorus of shouts
and yells, of cracking of whips and working of arms—
hero, then, though he may be, high though that number
nine be exalted, we see little here of the beauty and poetry
of the thorough-bred horse's life. We must seek this
rather in the sweet solitude of the downs and by-ways,
where the shepherd's hut is the ending-post, and the
farmer, thrice happy in his ignorance, will lean carelessly
on his stick as they march by, to ask "What's the name
of that 'un?"

[This sketch of Mr. Merry's racing stable at Russley was written in
the spring of the year 1862, when Thormanby, a winner of the Derby,
and Buckstone, a first favourite for the Derby, were both in work.]

JOHN GULLY.

In all the crowd of "characters" that have ever made up the ring on a race-course there were few more famous, and no one whose career has been so much of a romance, as that of John Gully. He was, indeed, essentially one of the men of his time, and the tyro or stranger-visitor would crave for a look at him long before his hero-worship centred on the Jockey Club lord or the leviathan leg. And yet Mr. Gully was by no means a remarkable man in his appearance; or, rather, in no way noticeable for the mere emphasis of his tone, or the quaint cut of his coat. With a manner singularly quiet, and almost subdued, he associated the air and presence of a gentleman, while his fine frame and commanding figure gave an innate dignity to his deportment that none who knew him would care to question. In fact, as your gaze rested on him, it was almost impossible to identify the man with the earlier stages of his history—the butcher's boy—the prizefighter—the public-house landlord—or the outside betting man. It was easier far to recognise him as a country squire of good estate, the owner of a long string of race-horses, or the honourable member of a Reformed Parliament. In a new country like America or Australia we can readily imagine that the fighting butcher might in due time develop into the stately senator; but here, in Old England, Mr. Gully's success is so far unparalleled. And he owed this not merely to his great wealth, but far more to his keen judgment, his good sense, and a certain straightforward respectability about everything he did. "The gentlemen," from the very first, took kindly to Gully, for they felt they could do so without any of the danger or disgust but too often resulting from the society of a self-made man. It must be our first business here to trace how he achieved that trying ascent in the world before him. Mr. Gully, then, was born at Wick-and-Abson, between Bath and Bristol, some time in the year 1783. He was brought up to the trade of a butcher, but very soon evinced a handiness in taking care of himself in sundry fistic tourneys with the joskins about home. This led to his visiting the metropolis, though with no very definite object beyond the practice of his trade, in which, however, he was not very fortunate, for soon after reaching his twenty-first year he was languishing in one of our London lock-ups as a prisoner for debt. His fellow-townsman, Pearce, better known as "The Chicken," came to see him there, when, to beguile the time, they put on the gloves for a bout or two. Gully did so well in this set-to that it came to be talked about, and ultimately he was liberated by the payment of the claims against him, and a match made with the Chicken, the latter staking six hundred to four hundred. The fight came off, after a disappointment in the July previous, at Hailsham, in Sussex, on October 8, 1805, when, after a very game battle, in which Gully received some fearful punishment, his friends interfered, and he was taken away in the fifty-ninth round, after one hour and ten minutes' hard fighting. Although beaten, Gully was by no means disgraced, and, in fact, he became not only a still greater favourite with the public, but on Pearce's retirement was offered the title of Champion of England, which, however, he resolutely declined. Prior to this offer, Gregson, a Lancashire man of immense size, and Gully's superior in height and weight, was bold enough to dispute the Bristolian's pretensions, and they met on October 14, 1807, in Six-mile Bottom, Newmarket, to contend for 200 guineas. Thirty-six rounds were fought with equal gameness on either part, and with almost equal punishment; but Gully got the last rally, and another knock-down blow rendered Gregson totally incapable. It was, however, a very near thing, and naturally enough the beaten man was anything but satisfied. Another match was consequently made for two hundred a side, which was decided on May 10, in Sir John Sebright's Park, in Hertfordshire, but after nothing like the struggle which signalised the first meeting of the men, as Gully from the first had it all his own way, his science and coolness completely out-generalling the wild rushes of his adversary. Seldom has any such an event attracted more interest, and on the Monday before the fight the good people of Bedfordshire, when they saw the crowds of strangers invading them, fancied the French had landed, and called out the volunteers! At the conclusion of this battle Gully publicly announced his intention of never fighting again, his left arm having received a permanent injury in his first and more formidable encounter with Gregson. *Boxiana* thus sums up his merits as a boxer: "Gully as a pugilist will long be remembered by the amateurs of pugilism, as peculiarly entitled to their respect and consideration; and if his battles were not so numerous as many other celebrated professors have been, they were contested with decision, science, and bottom, rarely equalled, and perhaps never excelled, and justly entitled him to the most honourable mention in the records of boxing. His practice in the art, it was well known, had been very confined, and his theoretical knowledge of the science could not have been very extensive, from the short period he had entered the lists as a boxer; but his genius soared above these difficulties, and with a fortitude equal to any man, he entered the ring a most consummate pugilist. In point of appearance, if his frame does not boast of that elegance of shape from which an artist might model to attain perfect symmetry, yet, nevertheless, it is athletic and prepossessing. He is about six feet high."

On leaving the Ring, Mr. Gully, like most successful pugilists, inclined to the public life of a Boniface, and was for some time landlord of " The Plough," in Carey-street, Lincoln's Inn Fields. But another ring found attractions for him, and he very soon devoted himself to the business of a betting man, though not always as a bettor round, or layer against horses. Indeed, at the Newmarket Craven Meeting, in 1810, when Lord Foley's Spaniard was got at by some of the Dan Dawson crew for the Claret, Mr. Gully was amongst those who turned round and laid the long odds on the favourite, upon whose defeat, it is said, his backer burst into tears, and declared he was a ruined man! However, in only two years subsequently—in 1812, that is—Mr. Gully had horses of his own, Cardenio being the first that ever ran in his name. He worked on gradually, still betting round, and at one period residing at Newmarket, with such tackle as Brutus, Truth, Rigmarole, Forfeit, Cock Robin, and others, until 1827, when he came prominently to the fore by the purchase of Mameluke, a horse that he gave Lord Jersey 4,000 guineas for, after his winning the Derby. How his new owner backed Mameluke for immense sums for the St. Leger, and how he was beaten by Matilda, after a fearful scene at the post, where Mr. Gully had himself to flog his horse off, are now matters of history. But, heavily as he had lost, the first man in the rooms, and the last to leave—never thinking of going, in fact, until every claim had been satisfied—was Mr. Gully. Sam Chifney, it will be remembered, rode the crack against Robinson on the mare; and Sykes had the care of the Derby winner at Hambledon. A year or two subsequent to this, Mr. Gully became the confederate of Mr. Ridsdale; and they opened well with Little Red Rover, who in 1830 ran second to Priam for the Derby. 'Thirty-two, however, was their great year, when the confederates won the Derby with St. Giles, and Gully the St. Leger with Margrave, John Scott having the preparation of the latter. Success, however, did not tend to cement the friendship of the two; and their quarrel came at last to a personal encounter in the hunting field, upon which Mr. Ridsdale brought an action, that terminated in a verdict, with £500 damages, against Mr. Gully, for the assault. This was not by any means the only serious altercation the latter was ever engaged in, as Mr. Osbaldeston once faced him with the poker in the Rooms at Doncaster, when "an explanation" ensued; and the currently-credited "meeting" was avoided. During this era in his history, Mr. Gully had purchased Upper Hare Park, near Newmarket, of Lord Rivers, where, as we have said, he for some time resided; but he sold this, in turn, to Sir Mark Wood, and bought Ackworth Park, near Pontefract—an accession which somewhat unexpectedly led to his representing that borough, in the Radical interest, for some sessions, in Parliament. He was twice returned, and on the first occasion without a contest. During his long sojourn here he also figured as a good man over a country, and as one of the chief supporters of the Badsworth Foxhounds. But the Turf, after all, was his ruling passion; and in 1834 he was heart and soul with the Chifneys, in their vain endeavour to win the Derby with Shillelagh, Gully offering Mr. Batson an extraordinary sum for Plenipotentiary as the horse was being saddled. He shifted later on, and for the last time, when he sent his horses to Danebury, where they did wonders for the rather falling fortunes of old John Day. There was the Ugly Buck to begin, with which they won the Two Thousand in 1844; and then, in the next year but one, Pyrrhus the First, and Mendicant, with which Mr. Gully won both the Derby and Oaks. Old Sam Day was his jockey; and we can recollect no more graceful illustration of the poetry of motion than that elegant horseman going up on that sweet mare, Mendicant. Everything was in unison, from the figure and style of the jockey, and the beautiful look of his filly, down to the very colour of his cap and jacket—the delicate violet, blended or mounted with white. They had brought out Weatherbit and Old England even before this; and in a few seasons more Mr. Gully matched them with another such a pair in The Hermit and Andover, the one a winner of the Two Thousand, and the other of The Derby. Rarely has any man enjoyed more signal success in his favourite pursuit; but, as we have said already, Gully owed much of this to his fine judgment, especially noticeable in the way in which he could reckon up a racehorse, or pick out a young one. Latterly, what with increasing years and failing strength, he had gradually declined, and, having sold Ackworth to Mr. Hill, had lived for some years at Marwell Hall, near Winchester, though he had still property in the North, including, we believe, some coal mines; and hence his death occurring at Durham: but he was buried at Ackworth on Saturday, March 14, 1863. He leaves a family of five sons and five daughters.

It was the late Mr. J. S. Buckingham, who, if we

recollect aright, when on a visit to Lord Fitzwilliam, tells of the impression made upon him by the appearance of a fine handsome gentleman coming up the staircase, with a beautiful girl in green velvet on either arm—the member for Pontefract, with two of his daughters. But, if we do borrow a sketch, it shall be from the pen of a sportsman ; and to no other could we be so indebted as to *Sylvanus*, who thus pourtrayed Mr. Gully in the very zenith of his career: "He had permanent lodgings at Newmarket, well and tastefully furnished, and dispensed his hospitality to his friends with no sparing hand. An excellent cook, claret from Griffiths, with an entertaining, gentlemanlike host, left little to be desired at the dinner awaiting us. Mr. Gully is justly esteemed, having raised himself from the lowest paths of life to the position not merely of wealth, but to that of intimacy amongst gentlemen, whether on or off the Turf, but still gentlemen in taste, which nought but the undeviating good manners and entertaining, unpresuming deportment of Gully could for a moment, or rather for any length of time beyond a moment, suffer them to tolerate. No man ever possessed these qualifications, gained through innate acuteness, great common sense, and a plastic disposition to observe and benefit by the chance *rencontres* with the courtly patrons of his day to a greater degree, taking the early disadvantages he had to contend with into consideration, than John Gully. No man could be more above pretence, or less shy at any allusions to his early and not very polished career, than himself. When I dined with him at Newmarket, as well as upon subsequent occasions, I was most gratified by this manly openness and lack of all sensitive, false shame, on any occasional appeal being made to the bygone. He, on the contrary, entered freely into many entertaining portions of his history, answered all my questions *con amore,* and with perfect good nature, as to the mode of training, hitting so as not to injure the hand, wrestling, and other minutiæ of the ring; passing the claret and slicing the pine, as if foaled at Knowsley or Bretby. He had a quiet, sly way of joking on any turf affair, on which, bear in mind, he was as *au fait* as Zamiel making a book for the Derby. The turbot came from Billingsgate by express, and the haunch from his own park. Moèt purveyed the champagne, Marjoribanks the port, and, as I have before said, Griffiths the Lafitte. We had no skulking host, be assured, but the most entertaining and liberal one alike." There is a genial tone about this sketch, that tells at once for its truth; and it would be difficult to give any man a better character. We ourselves have not attempted to blot out the earlier chapters in Mr. Gully's eventful life, feeling as we do that they only add point and force to the effect of his subsequent career. His position at every turn and phase of fortune was still a trying one; but no man more fairly earned the respect he gained. There is a very moral of good manners in such a man's history.

THE FARMER'S STORY.

"SECOND Class to Winchester!"

"*Ten-and-threepence*—there you have it!"

And I said "Thank you!" for the ticket, and the able-handed clerk said nothing for the money. In most commercial transactions the civilities generally come the other way; but railways are either exceptions to everything, or have started a new code of etiquette. I am inclined to lean to the latter opinion. It is a go-ahead no-time-for-nonsense age we live in.

I think it right to say I usually travel second class. I prefer it—that is, on the same terms with the gentleman who can always see and enjoy the play better from the forty-sixth row of the pit than he could from a front seat in the dress-circle; or, the other kind-hearted man who likes nothing so well as a mutton-chop dinner, though he could perhaps manage a basin of turtle, and the best side of a turbot, by way of a preface, if—they were not on the extras.

I am one of these—and so, with a stout heart and a small bag, I fight my way for a no-cushioned carriage. And yet, who says you don't meet with civility at a railway? Why, here is a zealous porter, finding me a window-seat at the remote end of a box, warranted free from draught, and from all "occasion" to change, and with a most commodious recess for my luggage safe under me. Mark how carefully John adjusts it! and with what a strange expression he half-eyes me, just as much as to say—

"Come, now; you know you ought to give me a shilling, because you know you ought not!"

There is no resisting such logic, and so I compromise myself and the matter with a four-penny-bit.

John looks me a thank'ee that I can't write.

Yes! of course, there is a gentleman's servant going to Southampton, and a soldier going to Gosport. I never saw a second-class carriage yet on this line without them. The contrast, too, is remarkably fine—the very genteel air of the one, and the rough-and-ready out-of-bounds bearing of the other. They are a long way off, though, this time; and I seem fated to run down with a full-blown old lady, who has spread out her black silk dress on the most unmistakable understanding of "there's no room here!"

But there is, still—at least, so thinks a fresh-coloured happy-visaged youngish gentleman, who tumbles himself in at the last moment with a bag, a rug, and a hamper, all at once, to the serious discomposure of the black drapery. He is a good-natured fellow, too; appears to think nothing of the little annoyance he has caused, but offers me a share of the rug with a ready-handed heartiness that might lead a stranger to think he had rather expected to find me there than not. By looks, and especially by his style of entering, I should say he was one of that doomed race—an agriculturist.

"Seen *Bell*, sir?" said the fated one, with a jolly smile running all over his face. It was a Saturday morning, I should say, and I was going to—well, never mind where, and never mind for what.

"Seen *The Life,* sir?" said he, pulling it out of his pocket, reeking wet with haste and news.

I had not, and preferred waiting for the usual Sunday morning, but was much obliged to him "all the same." The arrival took this as sociable, and after a very short spell at his paper broke out again—

"Seems to have had a good meeting at York, sir!"

It is an astonishing thing, certainly; but four-fifths of the people you meet now—pick them where you will—talk about racing: and I couldn't help saying as much in reply to the York commentary; but my new acquaintance took it good-naturedly enough.

"Why, I had a bit of a race-horse once myself, sir; and somehow or other I have had a turn for it ever since. A man, you see, who lives in the country, and whose business brings him every hour of his life amongst dogs and horses, can hardly help being a sportsman—at least, I know I could'nt, nor you either, I'm sure, by the look of you."

It seemed there was no use in attempting to deny so flattering an impeachment, and having accordingly at once owned to it, on went my friend faster than ever—

"Besides, I think gentlemen like to see their tenants with a good horse in their stable, and I always had one or two pretty fair. It was good fun, too, 'making' them, and paid as well when you came to part with them. At last, after I had been going on my own account for some six or seven years, I got hold of a little mare that promised even better than usual. She just could go a bit, and the best of them began to own it—so at last, near the end of the season, the gentlemen said I ought to get her ready for the Farmers' Cup. There were Hunt Races every spring, and a Farmers' Stake, of course; but somehow or other this farmers' race never seemed to be fairly won by a farmer. Lots of them tried for it at first, but a thorough-bred screw of some sort or other was generally smuggled into it, and the deuce a bit did the tenant, with the best horse, ever get the Cup to take home with him. Well, the gentlemen got quite as savage at this as we did; and so, when they found I had got a good mare, nearly all came to back me. The young squire—the son of him who kept the hounds—came himself every other day to lead me a gallop; and Sir William lent me one of his own lads out of the stables; and so away we went into regular training for it. The little mare stood it well, and looked, too, better and better every time she was out, so that by the end of the six weeks she was as 'fit as a fiddle,' as the jockeys say; and we really began to think about keeping the Cup where it was meant to be. There didn't seem much to be afraid of either. There were, to be sure, three of my own sort against me, but I knew I could run over them anywhere; and considering the twig we were in, there didn't seem much chance of their wearing us out any other way. There was one more, though, we couldn't say so much about—a great, big, ragged, one-eyed, varmint-looking, old beggar, that a draper in the town had picked up, or had sent him just within the three months. This draper was one of 'em that used to teaze us so much; held just fifty acres of land, to qualify him, it seemed; was a terrible chap for card-playing; and knew all sorts of dodges, and all sorts of people. Well, the gentlemen of course was dead against him, and talked of stopping him from running; but he'd got it all squared too well for that: so we had nothing to do but fight it out. I wasn't much afraid even of him either, though he'd got a regular deep-file to ride—a little quiet, civil, tea-drinking fellow, who called himself a gentleman-rider, but that nobody ever looked on as a gentleman still. He didn't seem to consider it so hisself, except when he had the cap and jacket on. However, you may be sure he was all right too—and so, away we went for the first heat.

"Well, the gentlemen said I wasn't to run for this, but to wait and see what the others was made off. The little chap on the one-eye'd-'un was to find this out too, but he went a very different way to work—ramming the spurs into Cheap Jack, as they called him, and going hard at it right away from the post. But I could have caught him still, if I had liked, for the little mare was pulling my arms off; and when he looked round at me once, I had a very good mind to go in at him. However, I didn't —and so on he went, and won easy—so they said, though his horse blew a smartish bit when he brought him back. The next heat it was my turn, and away I went, and he waited; and as one of the others was fairly distanced, another pulled up, and the third quite satisfied, we was left to have the last heat all to ourselves. Well, the gentlemen began to make quite sure now, and kept offering two and three to one against the other one; but old Calico and his party weren't half so bumptious as usual, and didn't seem to care about betting at all. So at last I got up for the "Who shall?" as proud as a peacock almost, for all the people kept saying, as I walked her down, 'Bravo, little May-Flower!' 'Well done, Blue Jacket!' and 'Well done, Master Stephen!' There was a goodish way to walk down for the start, and I had'nt got far before Mister comes trotting up to me on Cheap Jack, and smiling, and looking as civil as could be—

"'That's a neatish mare you have got there,' he says

after a bit, 'and mine ain't a bad bit of stuff either,' a-patting the old horse's lanky ribs.

"I didn't say much, so on he went again—

"'It seems almost a pity to run such a lot of these infernal two-mile heats for twenty or thirty pounds at most, and with a couple of nags, too, that might do a deal better.'

"'Ah!' says I, 'and what then?'

"'Why, just this,' says the little chap, a-coming close up to me, 'Why should we ride one another's horses' heads off, when we might come to an understanding, eh? Have just a bit of finish to please the clods—and what matter who wins, eh? Besides, only keep your mare fresh, and she's worth more over and over again to—'

"Just then the committee-man, who was to start us, rode up, and so being interrupted, the little man says to him—

"'Come, sir, I don't think we need trouble you; I reckon we can get off ourselves this time!'

"'Oh, do you?' says the other, a-boiling up, 'you'll go when I say *Go!* and not before. Be good enough to recollect as I'm the authorized starter, sir!'

"'Well, I hope *you* won't forget it, sir,' says he, laughing and winking at me, 'and now say *Go!* if you please, for we are ready.'

"'Go!' roars out the other, as if he was saying FIRE! to a regiment of soldiers, and Cheap Jack went off in a slow stiff canter, and I went after him.

*   *   *   *

"But I'm tiring you, sir," said my communicative friend, as a pull-up at one of the earliest stations rather checked the thread of his story, and sent the old lady's head out of window to make sure it wasn't "Portsmouth already."

"Not a bit!" I answered, "go on with the running—I'm watching it."

"Well, sir, on he went, and I after him, though I'll own I didn't know exactly my own mind—whether there was any *understanding* or what I ought to do. At any rate, I said to myself, I don't see why we *should* ride our horses' heads off; and when he does go faster, why I think I can go as fast as he can. So on we kept, hardly getting out of the canter; and as we went up the ropes the first time the folks were all holloing 'That's right, Blue Jacket! stick to him!' and I felt it was all right, too. But confound the fellow! I didn't stick to him either, as you'll see. Just about a quarter of a mile from home, or rather more, was the last turn—a little sharpish, into straight running; and as we were coming to it, I thought to myself, it's time to put the steam on a little now surely, when—*Bang!* I never see such a thing in my life!—he'd slipped the Lord knows how far away from me, all in a moment, and was working away at the one-eyed-'un like winking to make more of it. The old devil! too, was as game as a flint, and answered every dig like a good-'un, and spite all the bother I made on the little mare, I never caught him again, though we had a terrible flight for it as it was. A few strides more and I must have won.

"Well, I hardly ever saw such a row as there was afterwards; some swearing I'd sold the race, and threatening to duck me; others laughing, saying he'd been too much for me, and asking why I didn't ride in a wide-awake, and so on. But the gentlemen looked precious glum; while, as for me, I could have torn my eyes out, 'specially at the grand way the little chap took it all. He let the old horse—though he was pumped out as dead as a hammer—go nearly half round again before he stopped him, and then came back at last, patting his lanky ribs again, as if it was the horse and not the man as had won the race. He didn't say much either, only as he jumped down to weigh, to the people about him—

"'Come! they managed to make a tolerably good finish after all, didn't they?'

"Just as if he'd been cock-sure of winning all along—when he knew, as well as I did, that my mare could have run round him with fair play.

"Somehow or other, I couldn't face the Ordinary, and so, after bolting something by myself, I did what a good many men do when they don't know what to do with themselves—went to the play. When it was nearly over I walked back to the inn, and who should be standing at the door but my little friend, smoking a cigar—the first time I had seen him since the race. There he stood, looking as cool and quiet as ever. He made way for me, too, as civil as possible, but just as if he had never seen me before in his life. The end of it was, I was obliged to begin, and so I says at last—

"'Well, how about the stake—have you got it?'

"'Oh yes!' says he, as if a little surprised at my speaking to him. 'All right, thank'ee! I must say they pay much readier here than they do at many places I could name.'

"'I'm glad to hear that anyhow,' I went on, 'and of course our settling will be as easy.'

"'I beg your pardon, but I don't think I quite comprehend you?'

"'Why, what you said before running the last heat

about not wearing out our horses, as it didn't matter which won if we only had a good understanding between ourselves.'

"'Indeed!' says he, a-pulling away at his cigar, and speaking between his teeth, 'what then? what do you want then?'

"'Why *half*, of course,' I answers, a little riled at the way he was going on.

"'O! you do, do you?'' says he, bursting out laughing. 'You are a nice man, you are! And what for, I should like to know?'

"'What for! why hang it, you know I could have won if I'd liked!''

"'What! you lost on purpose, *eh?*—to get half when you might have had it all, *eh?* Well, that's a good one certainly, and very well tried on too; but it won't do here, my friend! Lost the race on purpose, *eh?*' and then he laughed again as if he had never heard of such a thing in his life, and the very notion rather tickled him.

"Well, I naturally got more savage at this, threatened to pitch into him, show him up, and so on; when, just as we was getting noisy, he pulls the cigar out of his mouth, and says, as cool as a cucumber, but as fierce as blazes still—

"'Now look here, young gentleman! if you want a row, *I*'ve no objection; but if I understand you correctly your argument is, that *you lost a race on purpose, and want to be paid for doing so—eh?* Is this the showing up you talk of? If so, go on; but as a man of the world, I should advise you not. It's a very good plant, I admit; but it won't do, I tell you; and as you may have a bit of a character here, it may be as well to keep it, *eh?* If *you **don't*** say anything more about it, *I shan't,* because it can't signify a rap to me any way; and, as a man of the world, I make it a rule to keep out of hot water if there's nothing to be got by getting into it. I'd advise you to do the same, and I wish you a very good night.'"

* * * * *

"Win-ches-ter—now then, who's for Win-ches-ter? No, marm; Winchester ain't Portsmouth—no, nor Southsea neither!"

MODERN HUNTING SONG.

"Bright chanticleer proclaims the morn"—
  By which he means to say
That those who do as their fathers did
  Will hunt by break o'day—
But we don't do as our fathers did,
  But quite the other way.

"At early dawn they met the morn,"
  As we learn from another chime;
And to get on the drag of the bold reyna
  Was what they voted prime—
But we look for a little more than that,
  All in the present time.

With many a cut at the cold sirloin,
  And a pull at the mightiest ale,
They hardened their hearts for the good ding-dong—
  Though their doings would hardly pale
The shy-fed, soda-watering youth,
  Who *now* o'er a country sail.

Then "one good horse would carry him,"
    As long as he liked to go;
And how this one would screw and creep,
    We all of us ought to know.
'Twas an amiable kind of thing no doubt—
    But wasn't it rather slow?

"There never were such times as those,"
    There never can be sure*ly*,
When a fox was gently simmer'd to death—
    Instead of this slap-bang fry,
That's turning him over and doing him brown
    Before he can wink his eye.

"Late hours, my lads, be sure to shun,"
    They are the root of many a sin;
All this cramming and racing is clearly come
    Of the time when we begin—
For our dear old dads were Hoiking home,
    When we're just 'Hoiking in!'

THE HARD-UP.

A RATIONAL EVENING'S AMUSEMENT.

One hears of so many different notions of hard-up, that it is difficult to say when you are or when you are not. This man is dreadfully hard-up with an over-bodied establishment and a three-thousand pounds butcher's bill; that one with a washerwoman's monthly reckoning and unrepaired boot-leather. Here is a poor fellow fearfully hard-up for something to do; there another equally so for somebody to be done; a third owns to be hard-up for somewhere to go; a fourth yet more so for something to go on. People, in short, are hard-up in most forms, and rarely with grateful stomachs, saving only the philosopher who cheerfully declared that he never felt down in the world, as he was always so very hard-up in it.

But let us look for a case or two in point, and let our first draw be over a bit of dinner. To achieve this, let us further lose ourselves in trying a new cut from Covent Garden to Piccadilly, and we may so, very likely, come to anchor at a demi-semi-English-French house that you could never have found by any other contrivance. We don't mean, mind, any popular well-known resort of Monsieur himself, where, with a wonderful foreknowledge of your coming and choice, they have everything cooked and kept hot for you two days at least before you arrive.

No, but a little quiet out-of-the-way house, where you may see some very varmint gentlemen, awfully up to what's what and who's who, and get a fresh bit of fish, and a chop disguised any way you like, almost as cheap as at the veriest make-shift in Newgate-street. We will say no more, or the place will get appreciated and crowded—and that, of course, means spoilt—so tumble up-stairs, and "give your orders" at once; for, strange as it may sound, they will keep you waiting here for your dinner while they dress it.

Stop! did'nt I tell you so!—Table of three on the other side of the room—Youngish, fastish, but still gentlemanly lad of seventeen or eighteen; jolly, stout, dark, curly-haired gentleman of forty; and long-faced, thin, quiet, " I-can-lay-it-you" looking one, of any age from five-and-twenty to seven-and-thirty you may like to set him at. Hark!—

"Well, but I say, Billy, why did'nt you go to the Masquerade?" an inquiry apparently repeated from the jovial one to the juvenile.

"Because I was so jolly hard-up, I tell you. I had'nt enough by three-and-sixpence to pay for a ticket; and Weyton, who was the only fellow who would lend it me, hadn't got it."

"That was hardish-run, too," said the Hyperion-headed gentleman, with a laugh; "but what did you do with yourself?"

"I didn't know what to do with myself—that was it; thought about Hungerford Bridge after dinner, and all that sort of thing; when just as I was in the middle of a debate, and in the middle of a street, I was precious nearly saved the trouble of all further discussion by being run into, as near as a toucher, by one of the ' ROYAL BLUES'

—that blessed kind of conveyance whose boast and glory it is to charge you 'only 4d. all the way!' Egad, says I, I'll be booked for Chester Square."

"Who's there, Billy?"

"The aunts, you know; elderly maiden ladies, living in retirement; two or three hundred dozen of tea-spoons with the family crest; £5,000 in five-pound each North Riding notes; butler — an aged elderly man, faithful but unfortunately deaf, sleeping for safety in a room where nobody can find him, and all that sort of thing."

"But I say, my young friend," joined in the I-can-lay-it-you looking youth, "you should have gone there before—a wide-awake bird like you, too."

"'Bless your innocent heart,' as Cabby says, I'd been there too often; tired 'em out; had to ask for something to drink; was supposed to smell of smoke, and look 'wild'; never got a screw out of either of them during the eighteen months I had been in town. Had I not an income of eighty per annum in a government office, with a fair chance of promotion—perhaps a little assistance from my father, though that could hardly be required—and so forth?—No, all I ever got to carry away was a pot of marmalade, and *The Young Man's Best Friend.*"

"Well, that was handsome, too; and what did you do with them?"

"Why, *The Young Man's Best Friend* I made a present of to a young woman I met in Piccadilly, under the notion that he ought to be as good a friend to her as he was to me; and the marmalade I made a bargain about with a 'poor b'y' selling lucifers—namely, that he was to set-to and clear out the whole pot at once. He was awfully hard-up, but I'll be shot if Aunt Mary's 'making' did'nt beat him, for, after forcing very strong running for about half way, he threw up his head and cut it. 'It's so sticky, sir,' says he, in a voice that seemed affected by a cold he had caught the winter but one before last, and never quite got rid of again—'It's so sticky, sir; I must have a drop of water to finish him off with.'"

There was a tolerably loud laugh at the 'poor b'y's' expense; and another drop of something-and-water being ordered to drink his health, the open-hearted Billy proceeded:

"However, down I went again to Chester Square, looking deuced old, as you may fancy; but I'll be shot if that did'nt do it. I was 'looking quite steady' and 'altered'; and it was, 'William will have some tea?' and 'a glass of wine to Mr. William'; till at last, by Jupiter! the old ladies came to the conclusion that Her Majesty's Government was over-working me, and that I wanted some relaxation."

"Heaven bless them!" said the stout man, with a sigh; "couldn't you spare such an aunt, Billy—one out of two, you know?"

"Not exactly. However, on they went, warming up to the collar, till at last they proposed and seconded it that 'I ought to be taken somewhere that very evening.' 'Bravo! Billy,' says I to myself, 'surely the old ladies will never be game enough to take you to the Masquerade, after all.' I daren't hint it, but there I sat and hoped. Carriage ordered. On I went with them—at waiting orders, you know—keeping close up to their heads, but never getting right in front; and where do you think they took me to, after all?"

"Can't say, I'm sure," replied the I-can-lay-it-you, seeming as if he really was calculating what he ought to offer about it.

"To the Judge-and-Jury, perhaps?" said the other, with his usual grin.

"To the POLYTECHNIC!" burst out Billy in a scream; and the young reprobate laid his head on the table, and laughed till he cried at the very notion of having been provided with an evening's amusement at that justly celebrated exhibition of art and science.

"They did, by Jupiter!" he went on, when his mention of the fact would allow him to proceed: "Great guns there, too; regular subscribers; gave me a personal introduction to the Diving Bell, who took off his helmet to show he was mortal, and looked 'beer' at us; but I was too hard-up, and Aunties of course did'nt understand him."

"Many people there, Billy?"

"Oh, lots, of a sort, you know; ladies in spectacles; servant-gals in their second-best shawls and every-day dresses; and 'well-read' looking men in white ties, which no doubt *had been* uncommon smart on Sunday."

"See anybody you knew?"

"Yes! I'll be dashed if I did'nt! old 'Punctuality White' in our department, that slow-and-sure-coach, who does everything by rule; dinner, half-an-hour to eat it; quarter-of-an-hour to read the paper and chew the cud; ten minutes to reckon up within himself the score, before he asks the waiter, in an awfully grand way, 'what's to pay?'"

"By himself?"

"Oh, no!—elderly lady, who somehow or other had managed to 'smug' in her umbrella, and was hugging it for very life; and young swell of six or seven, in Charles the Second hat, very 'heavy' great coat, and Flying Dutchman plaid gaiters. And there was Old Punctuality doing the polite in the most expensive style—explaining the principles of electricity: If you want to be 'shocked,' touch the conductor; if you don't, leave him alone; and if you fancy you are hurt, there's no extra charge for holloaing—a privilege the Dutchman at once availed himself of by kicking up a most awful row directly he and the conductor became acquainted."

"Well, and was there anything else to see, Billy?"

"I believe you there was—all sorts of games, only it seems a standing order of the place that you must be 'sold.' If you are up-stairs a bell rings all in to begin, and you are told to go down; if down, *vice versâ*, and you go up. But Aunty was up and down to all their schemes. First of all, the Ballad Music of England, with illustrations."

"What! the ballet, and ballet-girls! that must have been worth seeing?"

"No, no! the *ballad*-music—gentleman talks till he's tired, then sings, then tells a story, then sings again. 'Twasn't bad; only he did it all in such a lackadaisacal, die-away fashion, as if he was going off for instant execution at the end of the entertainment. Indeed, when he came to introduce a ballad he'd had the extreme misfortune to compose himself, and that had inflicted the further inexpressible agony on him of becoming rather popular, I thought his dejection would get too much for him, and we should have to stop the piece."

"No such luck, I reckon, Master William?"

"No! so then we toddled off again to the Chemistry —more interesting; which means, a vast deal slower. Lecture on Ancient Agriculture, when they used to make their ploughshares red-hot to get them easier into the ground—at least, so I took it. Red-hot shares introduced, and 'my assistant,' to show that by practice the ancient ploughboys didn't care a rap about 'em, hot or cold, ordered to take his shoes and stockings off, and march away forthwith. 'My assistant'—a fat-headed boy, with a very groggy, chilblainy pair of pins—takes his 'walk-over' accordingly, though he looked uncommon like breaking down at every stride."

"Perhaps that was why they *fired* him?" said the calculating gentleman, in so serious a tone that it was some time before they honoured his joke by taking it.

And so Billy went through that wonder to him—a rational evening's amusement, winding up with dissolving-views, and "the best sort of a target for a snap shot he ever saw." Previous to this, though, the old ladies had stood some cherry-brandy in the refreshment-room, where "we found the Dutchman all alone, cocked up on a chair, and eating a bath bun at the rate of a mouthful in half-an-hour—evidently discussing to himself the principles of electricity, and connecting in his own mind the crack he got on the fingers with some proceedings under water on the part of my friend in the Castle of Otranto helmet."

"Well," he went on, "at last it seemed about all over: the white neckcloths, 'as wos,' made a terrible rush for the umbrella-stand, and the servant-gals began to think it was 'past ten o'clock.' Just then Aunt—the longer one in the tooth, that is—began to get rather uneasy, staring away at the Humbugasoi under the glass cases, and fumbling away like mad all the time at her bag. 'In course' we left her to herself; and just then Mary, who always *seemed* like a good 'un, slipped a couple of sovereigns into my hand, with a 'William, don't mention this; only mind and be prudent, there's a good boy!'"

"I'd hardly time to pocket them before up sails the

other, looking two or three sizes larger than life; and 'William!' says she too."

"What, another couple, eh, Billy? Egad! you was in luck for once."

"No, no, hear me out—and 'William,' says she, 'I have watched you narrowly here to-night, and admired the interest you have taken in everything—there, William, is a perpetual admission, which will allow you to come and improve yourself as often as you choose.'"

"My wig! what a sell!" said the stout man, with a roar; "and did you take it?"

"To be sure I did; handed them into the carriage; bid them good night; got all sorts of blessings and advice in return; and hailing a Hansom, was at the Albion, in Drury-lane, at a quarter before twelve!"

"And do you mean to say you went to the Masquerade, after all?"

"To be sure I did: and let fellows say what they will about the Masquerade being slow—perhaps it is, in some cases—after a jolly night with four or five good fellows, who go there with the may-be mistaken notion of getting something a great deal better; or, after leaving a lot of nice girls with the same idea; or, rushing away from single-handed lodgings, under the plea that you must be delighted forthwith. I would'nt warrant it then exactly —but try it, as I did, my friends; let it come unhoped for after a first heat at the Polytechnic, or the Rev. Mr. Grind at Exeter Hall—by Jove! I never had such a night in my life, and I don't think Her Gracious Majesty's Ministers had much out of me the next day."

"Melt the two, Billy?"

"Rather! and what d'ye think I did with the Perpetual Order?"

"Don't know, I'm sure."

"Made a bargain with a cabby to take me home for that and a shilling; and now No. 5,956 can strut in and shake hands with the Diving Bell, and inspect the Humbugasoi whenever he likes."

"Hang it! but that was rather a bad compliment to Aunty, too, Billy?"

"Well, perhaps it was; but then, what was I to do, you know? I was so jolly HARD-UP!"

OLD JOHN DAY.

ANOTHER link in Turf history is lost to us. It would seem, indeed, as if the chain were giving way altogether in a place or two. Take ten, or twenty, or even thirty years since, and what a group could we picture, as the bell rang for saddling for the opening race over Bath, Bibury, or Cheltenham! Here, inside the ropes, waiting for his horse, is quaint, quiet, Jem Chapple, in the well-worn white body and red sleeves of Isaac Sadler, who in his own favourite body clothes, the blue coat and brass buttons, is finally determining whether they shall "go for the heat" or not. Close at their elbow stands his namesake, Isaac Day, of Northleach, amply protected against the Lansdowne breezes in his well-cut drab dreadnought, and the as invariable drab trowsers to match. In earnest converse with him mark the useful "Vicar," or dandy Arthur Pavis, come all the way from Newmarket to ride Caravan for the Cup; while sedately jogging up on his hack, hails them "Honest John" himself, looking as grave as a parson, and very like one, even when he was stripped to the strictly clerical habiliments of Mr. Wreford—black jacket and white cap—who is going to win the Two Year Old with Wapiti, Westeria, or to put some other such invincible "a double" on them.

And have they all gone from amongst us? Shall the starting signal summon them no more? The only echo is *no more!* No more shall the one Isaac bustle away on his varmint pony, or the other walk calmly back into the

Stand to watch a Delightful or a Designful sweep by under the delicate handling of careful Jemmy. *No more* shall " the Vicar " fairly thrash out his fiver in the *second, first, third*, and *first*—that ultimately lands it. *No more* shall natty Arthur give even Mr. Peyton himself a wrinkle in the way of a good get up, or "Honest John" save the Two Year Old by a head, and win the Guineas in a canter on Little Red Rover, with all the staid propriety and decorum so befitting such an occasion. They are gone! In but a brief season or so, Chapple, Wakefield, Isaac Sadler, Isaac Day, and at last "Old" John himself, have fallen, as it were like ninepins, one over the other.

But amongst them all there was no such a remarkable man as the one whose career stands as a heading to this paper. It was not merely as a jockey of local repute that John Day was celebrated, not chiefly from winning on his own horses over his own ground. He could follow Chapple back to Newmarket, and try his head and hand successfully against the Buckles, Chifneys, and Robinsons over that classic heath. He could face the howling wilderness of Epsom, and out-general the canny north-countryman in his own home, and outlast him for the very race of his heart. Perhaps, however, after all, it is not as a rider of horses so much that John Day's name will live. We question greatly whether the majority of sportsmen would not be more inclined to honour him in another branch of the science, and to pit him rather against John Scott the trainer than William Scott the jockey. In point of fact, he long stood the ordeal of this comparison, and when Malton began to threaten, people instinctively turned to Danebury for the answer. The two Johns knew well enough how often the strength of their strings and the knowledge of their business got them nominations in this forced handicap.

Let us see how far the *Stud Book* and *Calendars* warranted the heavy responsibility with which the world so long saddled "Honest John." Without the one at our elbow we should say he was at his decease, within four or five years or so of the "age" of man; or, in other words, that he had seen somewhere about sixty-six summers. He was very well bred for his profession, as his father was a country trainer of some repute; but as "Nimrod" wrote of him five-and-twenty years since, in his famous *Quarterly Review* article, "The endowments of Nature are not always hereditary, and well for our hero that they are not, for he is the son of a man who weighed twenty stone, whereas he himself can ride seven stone." The father lived at Houghton Down, where John was born, and his mother, a Miss Barham, came of a very good family at Stockbridge—as many would say, of a much superior one to that of her husband. Hence the son's second name, John Barham Day; a title, though, that he never took up in full until his son, again, "Young John," had set up in business on his own account. It would be idle, however, to attempt to identify John Day as *the* son of his parents, or yet as their son the jockey. Old Mrs. Day, his mother, and herself as good a judge of what a horse could do as one-half the professors, was fond of telling the story of a race she once saw, in which *five* of her own boys rode. These were—John Barham; the far more elegant and accomplished Sam; Charles, who subsequently went to Russia; William; and James, a veterinary surgeon, at one time in practice near Exeter, but latterly living with his nephew William, at Woodyates. We do not remember that the old lady ever pointed the story by adding the name of the winner. It will be seen from this that John began life with all the incentive to excel that even the rivalry of his own family could conduce to. He increased this wholesome stimulus on the first available opportunity by paving the way to a family of his own. In other words, he married at a very early period in his career. The partner of his choice was also from the neighbourhood of Stockbridge, but the match was terribly against his father's wishes, to whom he was naturally becoming very useful. Of course the lad had been almost altogether home educated, while one of his first engagements " out " was encouraging enough. It was with no less a personage than His Majesty King George the Fourth, at that time Prince of Wales, for whom he rode light weights. The King, indeed, never forgot him, and only two years before the Royal George's decease, that is in 1828, John had the honour of riding his favourite mare, Maria, for the Somersetshire, at Bath, at that time a race of some importance, and which he won. But even under the countenance of Royalty it must not be supposed John Day fell into all these fine doings at once. Like most of the jockeys of those days—the provincials especially—he had a hard apprenticeship to serve. There was no winning at York one afternoon, and at Abingdon the next; but the practitioner methodically went the circuit, with the saddlebags and his hack—riding heat after heat, and taking, perhaps, at best but two or three small fees, strictly *à la carte*, in a day. Still John's good name and steady, sober conduct served to smoothe the way for him; and the Duke of Grafton, one of his firmest patrons, at length sent him a " special retainer " to come to Newmarket. It might have been difficult for John Day himself to have dated many of his first successes, and at the opening of his history the public records did not deign to do as much for him. However, as far back as the autumn of '22, more than forty years since, we find him at Newmarket, in the First October Meeting, winning the Trial Stakes on Guerilla for his grace of Grafton, beating amongst others Gustavus, the Derby winner of the year previous. Sam Chifney finishes first for the next thing on; and then, in the Houghton, "J. Day" again claims a Match on Mystic for Mr. Batson. He gradually got at home here after this, and carried the scarlet livery across the Flat in many a close encounter. With the riding of such a stable he was naturally up in most of the great races, and after a taste of the Two Thousand, and the Thousand Guineas, which he won in the same year, 1826, on Dervise and Problem, he fairly matriculated at Epsom in 1828, where he carried off the Oaks for the Duke on Turquoise, with 25 to 1 against her. Only three years later he arrived at what must still be considered the *acmé* of his career as a jockey. He again won the Oaks for the Duke on Oxygen, after what was generally admitted to be a most brilliant display of horsemanship. In the same season he landed his first Leger for the then Lord Cleveland, on the outsider Chorister; while he was anything but idle in his own district. One of his favourite nags, Mr. Biggs' Little Red Rover, was just then in full sail, and John was winning a Plate at Blandford on him this week, the Guineas and a Purse somewhere handy the next, the Cup at Cheltenham, a handicap at Bath, and so on. He was a terrible teaser to the Day, Dilly, Sadler School, and in his last season, when six years old, John flew the Little Rover at even higher game. He accepted for the Goodwood Stakes with him, and won it on him. By the turn of another still succeeding year he had again carried off his favourite race, the Oaks, for Mr. Cosby, on Pussy; and this landmark at once leads us to the great era in John Day's life as a jockey and trainer—his connection with Lord George Bentinck. When that grand meteor gradually shone forth upon the hemisphere, John Day was his attendant satellite. It was John who advised, who trained, who rode, who bought, and who betted. It was John Day who vanned Elis into Doncaster, and courted Fortune with a bold stroke for success that was fated, alas! never again to be so realised in such a conjunction. In vain the string was increased. In vain that the nominations swelled the pages of the *Calendars*, or that investments followed in the books of the industrious. Too late was it that simple Mr. Bowe bloomed forth into Lord George himself, or that the good Duke of Portland came to understand, in jockey-boy lingo, "who belonged to all these horses." It was a dashing game to play, too! and what a stand they made on the first trump card they drew! How well we yet remember Grey Momus' race for the Derby! How the crowd took to him, and cheered him, and singled him out at "the corner" and roared "the Grey! the Grey!" till they could roar no more. And while John was rolling about on *his* rolling tired horse, how close and quiet an old acquaintance, one Mr. Chapple sat, knowing he had got the length of him, and knowing—as no one ever did better—that he had only to bide his time to win. And then popularity veered round like the weathercock it is, and the poor grey was led off without a soul to sympathise with him, while shouts rent the air again and again for "Sir Gilbert!" But Grey Momus was not half a bad horse either. In a week or so we saw him win the Ascot Cup with "little

Billy Day" on him against Epirus and Caravan; and on Lord George's own cherished course at Goodwood he ran home first, for both the Racing and Drawing-room Stakes. There was yet better to come. There was to be one brilliant flash before the display was over, and John worked it up with Crucifix. She did all he asked her, and that was no little—went triumphantly through her two-year-old engagements—just saved the Oaks—and then "the clipper," though she kept her flag flying for a while, was virtually out of commission. But so it ever has been, and ever will be with our modern race-horses, which only do more in a few months than their illustrious sires ever accomplished in a lifetime. Close a thing as this was, "Honest John" had got his hand in for the Oaks again the year previous, when Fulwar Craven, being scarcely susceptible of his own trainer's qualifications as a jockey, as evinced in the Derby, changed John Day for him in the Oaks, and Deception won as she liked. For a season or two more the tide blew dead against the Bentinck venture, and at length Lord George sat him down in melancholy mood, and said, "My racing establishment costs me eight thousand a year, and I can't win a fifty." Ill fortune, as usual, led on to disputes and dissensions, and my Lord and John Day parted anything but the friends they should have done.

There was to be no *integratio* to the *amantium iræ*. On the contrary, the feud raged with all the proverbial acerbity of a civil war. Lord George declared himself not so much at variance with John as against the whole of the Day family. But the father warmly espoused his own people's cause, and the great battle of Gaper, as historians will tell us hereafter, was fought on the downs at Epsom in the summer of 1843. John Day felt "the leggy brute" could not win, and gradually "went on" until he was full forty thousand against him. My Lord, on the other hand resolutely brought his horse to a shorter and shorter price, till there was no "getting out." Often, though, as the story has been told, and much as has been made of it, no one ever told it like poor "Sylvanus."

"Now let us take a peep at the Corner on the Sunday.

"'What's Gaper's price?' said a very distinguished handsome-looking fellow of the true English countrified cut of a gentleman—a cut, let me tell you, it is in vain to look for in any other part of the world that I ever saw. Consummate cleanliness, joined to exquisite taste in dress, is the peculiar feature that strikes you; the gentle voice, quiet composed manner, and harmonious natural look, add a charm and a finish to the beauty of countenance that is certainly only found in the higher classes in England.

"However, 'What's Gaper's price?' inquired the tall man in leather trowsers, a maroon double-breasted coat, with Club buttons, and large fawn-coloured cravat; 'I've not quite done yet, and can take the odds to a thousand.'

"'Beggar my looks,' said a little *very anxiously smiling* elderly man, in long gaiters, and black frock coat of the old chaise-driver or Sir Tatton's length of flap; 'this is coming it too strong to be pleasant. I'm clear forty thousand agin him!'

"'What'll you take, my Lord?' asked Sunflower; 'I'll lay you five thousand to two that Cotherstone beats him.'

"'Thank ye; it will not suit my purpose. I'll take six thousand to one outright.'

"'Beggar his long limbs!' said the little old fellow in the jarvey's coat; 'he'll make his spindle-shanked brute first favourite yet. I must get Gully to see him before he springs to even betting—though he has no more chance on his merits than a man in boots.'"

How capital it all is! What a famous photograph is that of Lord George, and how good the "anxiously smiling" John! And somebody does *see* him, and John is permitted to get part of it "off" at last. And "Black Bill" strips for the grand magnificent Cotherstone, though they have one of the finest horsemen of his age in Sam Rogers against him. The two Johns are right, however. Scott knew his horse was good enough, and Day felt the other was not. But he finishes well up, and John heaves a heavy sigh of relief as he vows never to take such liberties again.

There is another era approaching by this, as another leviathan is landed on the short green turf. The brothers John and Alfred are pulling famously together at Danebury, while William is developing into a great man all by himself in Wiltshire. And so, when "Mr. Howard" is announced, "Honest John" readily gives him the interview, and has once more a long string in work. He is now only trainer, for John Day is getting on, and to Tiny Wells is entrusted the handling of them. This is too recent a chapter in modern history to require long dwelling on. But Virago, saved to her third year, fairly swept the country, north and south. Then, there were Scythian, and Little Harry, and Queen's Head, and Oulston, and others, all speaking to the stuff left in old John, and that yet to come on in young Wells. Nevertheless, in the summer of '55 John Day withdrew somewhat suddenly from Mr. Howard's service, left Findon, and with a comfortable competence settled himself with his son William at Woodyates. He died here, after having been indisposed for some time, on Wednesday, March 21, 1860.

There are few public men in his way of life who had more peculiarities, or were better known on a race-course. It was, in fact, impossible to mistake "Honest John" on his horse. He had a very noticeable hollow in the back, good width of shoulder, and that peculiar cast of countenance there was no mistaking. He was altogether a well-made little man, but he was scarcely ever a great horseman. There are comparatively few brilliant bits associated with his name. He rather wanted style, too, particularly in his set-to; but he was a careful, safe man, and seldom made a mistake. Still, we repeat, it is as a trainer that John Day will be remembered. There was no better judge of a young one, and no one knew better what to do with him, *if* he could only stay to learn all John could teach him. His preparation was proverbially severe, and not many could stand it.

"Well, John," said Isaac Sadler to him one day, as the former was watching three of his two-year-olds at exercise—"Well, John, what do you think of them?"

John "beggared his looks," and hinted something not very complimentary.

"Ah, never mind," answered Isaac; "I will tell you what they *have* got, John—they have got twelve sound legs amongst them, and that's more than you can count amongst your fifty up there."

On another occasion, John himself asked a friend's opinion of five youngsters of Lord George's that had just come up from Doncaster.

"Why, they won't stand your training a fortnight," blurted out the other.

"*My* training! what d'ye mean by that, sir?"

"Well," said his companion, softening it down a bit, "I think the Danebury Hill will be a *leetle* too much for them."

And sure enough in a fortnight two of the Velocipedes had thrown out curbs! But find a clipper to face the "Danebury Hill," and he was sure to come in the market. Despite the pot that now and then boiled over, people knew this, and treated the stable, even in its most fanciful of humours, with a certain degree of respect. John Day was always well backed. "The gentlemen" generally liked him, and, from our present Premier downward, he held many staunch friends. He won the Cesarewitch for Lord Palmerston with Iliona, a race rendered amusingly remarkable by the controversy over the iota and omega. The colours he looked himself most at home in were the "all scarlet" of the Duke of Grafton, the black with the white cap of Mr. Wreford, the green with the red cap of Mr. Biggs, the light blue and white cap of Lord George Bentinck, and it would be hardly right to omit the pink and black stripe of Lord Cleveland. Abraham Cooper, the Royal Academician, had more sittings at him than any other artist, and painted him successively on Elis, Deception, and Crucifix. The most successful portrait, however, was one in a family picture painted by the same artist, by order of Lord George Bentinck, who presented it to John Day with the understanding that it was to descend to his eldest son. In this group John stands in his great coat by the side of the mule phaeton, in which are seated his wife and his mother, while his son Sam is mounted on the game Venison, and William on Chapeau

F

d'Espagne. The picture was exhibited in the Royal Academy, where, as we well remember, it attracted much attention from all classes of visitors.

"A Family Picture" for John Day would have required a much fuller canvas to have done him thorough justice. He had in all, we believe, twelve children by his first wife, but none by the second. These included quite another generation of jockeys. There was "Young John," a powerful, resolute horseman in his time, who rode in the Grand Steeple Chase over the Vale of Aylesbury, and whose courage and coolness tackled so successfully with Grey Momus, a very violent, hard-pulling brute, in the days of his hot youth. Then comes poor Sam, a boy blessed far beyond his fellows with that inestimable virtue called patience. William Day was never quite meant for a jockey, and it is commonly a joke against him whenever he puts himself up; but he has amply proved his talent as a trainer. The flower of the flock, however, as a horseman, is or *was* the all-accomplished Alfred, who unites in a singularly happy degree the graces and the uses of his art. Another brother, Henry, is in the law; Edward was manager of the Warfield Paddock; while one of the daughters is married to William Sadler, and another to Mr. Dixon, who at one period held rather a prominent position on the Turf.

Few men led so generally a steady life as the late John Day. He went to church regularly twice every Sunday, and was somewhat demonstratively devotional in his habits. He was fire-proof against the many temptations of the race-course, the winning money, and the good company; but he liked his joke either with or against him; and *Bell's Life* has told all the world over how his horse cried "per-quavi," and how the civil gentleman who lost

the "pony" to him "never came anigh" afterwards!
Still he was always a curious contrast to many of
his fellows—grim Sam Chifney, smart, cheerful *Mr.*
Conolly, or *ou*dacious Bill Scott. What a time it
must have been when he found Coronation satisfied,
and half the town and trade of Oxford ruined—with
"Sweet William" slanging him alongside on Satirist,
"Does he pull you *now*, John?" "Beggar your looks,"
John must have answered if he could have said anything,
as he tried to pull the slashing son of Sir Hercules together for a final effort. But they are both gone, and before
them how many that might help to tell the story of
"Honest John's" eventful and respectable life. Goodison,
Arnull, Clift, Wheatley, and Chifney herald him on Newmarket Heath in an age all but passed away; while Wells
may still talk over his leg up to Virago, or "Young
John" dwell on the lingering fondness of the old gentleman for giving them "a spin."

THE PRIVATE PUPIL.

(FROM THE DIARY OF A. SOFTUN, ESQ.)

When I was a *very* young man—and that is not such an extraordinary time back either—I had the peculiarly good fortune to pass my state of transition under the immediate care of the very reverend as well as learned Dr. Gradus. This happy era in life's journey every one must have some recollection of—the time when you are not *quite* responsible for your own acts, but feel quite equal, nevertheless, to go with the best of them.

The Doctor's domestic circle was limited, which of course went to imply that his terms were not. In fact, things were done altogether with rather a high hand; and so, when my good mother ventured to hint somewhat nervously that horse-exercise would tend much to increase my bodily health, as well as materially add to my appetite for Greek Play, not the slightest objection was offered to so reasonable a suggestion. The Doctor had a capital stable, a groom who had lived some years with "Sir Richard," and perfectly understood his business—in a word, there was every disposition to make us both comfortable; and on the same night I took possession of my bed-room, my "riding-horse"—as he was modestly designated— took possession of his box.

He was rather an imposing-looking hack, too—fifteen-three good, well furnished throughout, legs as clean as a foal's, and seven off. My own experience, too, went to assure me that he was something more than a hack; and after I had cut in once or twice with the harriers, there were plenty of others willing to believe as much. Indeed, I heard one oracle, of rather a serious turn of mind, acknowledge the fact with a "what a pity !" kind of commentary—meaning, of course, what a sad thing it was that so good a horse should come to be rattled about by a young gentleman of such primitive notions as myself. I can't say, though, that I saw the thing altogether in this light.

Within a fair walk of the vicarage there had been providentially provided a good-sized country town, whither we went to buy sticks, post letters, have our hair cut, and get through any other trifling business of a bye-day. By the end of the first season my horse's reputation was in very strong bloom here; and when, in accordance with the especial spirit of the times, a steeple-chase fever broke out amongst the inhabitants, they registered a half-promise from me that my nag should "make one." I was very young at the time—a fact which any gentleman who may have the "what a pity !" conclusion again ready for use will please to remember.

The attempt prospered : the cheque of a decidedly sporting banker was already good for the "fifty added," and the day of entry drew on. Unfortunately, as it would seem, just at this very nick of time a veterinary surgeon, of acknowledged ability, fancied that my "riding horse" had got a little heat in one of the back-sinews, and, with the Doctor's permission, took him off to his own hospital, the more effectually to put him on his legs again. The way he set about this was certainly rather extraordinary; but it only shows the great advance we have made in the development and practice of veterinary science. The very next morning he gave the grey a stiffish gallop of nearly four miles, and within a day or two one yet more severe—a system further persevered with, and only relieved occasionally by a scurry over the country. There appeared, though, no reason to quarrel with the course of treatment adopted, for the horse looked all the better for it; and as the back-sinew got no worse than it had been, there was little to complain of on that score.

In fact, I am afraid, my hack from the first was treated more as a private pupil than a hospital patient, and we were in high spirits at the nomination—a little toned-down, however, by a written entry, all the way from London—"*br. h.* THE WEAVER"—who had won twice already that season, and that we certainly did not suspect would have honoured us with his presence on the occasion. A couple of the Doctor's select circle, I should say, had contrived to reach the Black Lion that evening—myself and a senior pupil, who had proved on one or two opportunities occurring, that he was, as they say, "a few pounds better" on a horse than I could qualify to. It was by his hand, indeed, that the back-sinew recipe had been generally applied; and, as the Vet. himself confessed it was as good as a sermon to see him screw through a queer place, The Weaver threat settled it, and my friend Archy, having made up his mind on the matter long before, consented to take my place and ride the chase.

It is the fashion to say you cannot half enjoy any kind of amusement without you take a very active part in what is going on. I only know that I never relished a farce so little as when I attempted "Robin Rough-head," or felt so thoroughly miserable and disgusted with myself as when, in the excess of my happiness and satisfaction, I had to kick over the table, and "d—n the doomplings!" The excitement, then, of owning a race-horse, coupled with the further piece of luck of running him on the sly, was, as may be imagined, quite sufficient for my young idea, and I was well content enough to watch Archy get out, and in order, a pair of wonderfully well-cut leathers, with boots almost as good, and a "blue body with red sleeves," that his "governor had lost many a hundred on." In short, the old gentleman had spent all he could in supporting the national sport; and so his son, of course, was very well grounded to take a leading part in so all-engrossing a sort of manly recreation.

Thursday morning found us once more at the Black Lion on another hair-cutting expedition. Here rumour said that the field would not be a strong one, but the line would; that the Weaver party were in great force, and that the race was going all one way. I heard this rather oddly confirmed myself, while waiting in the coffee-room for Archy, who had retired to don the immaculate boots and breeches. For some little time I had it all to myself, but was at length intruded on by a couple of gentlemen who had evidently come in to talk business. At first they seemed half inclined to leave me in undisturbed possession; but supposing, no doubt, there could be nothing to fear from a fresh-coloured, good-looking youth in white cord trousers and a blue monkey-jacket, they made good their point, and walked in, while I went on with my divided occupation of looking out of the window and grinding a tooth-pick. I did not listen, but I could hardly help gathering something of this from the observations of the shorter man of the two, who spoke in a tone offensively confident, and looked, in a suit of seedy black, like an undertaker's man out for a holiday :— "The chase was all *squared*; The Weaver was *meant*; and as for the others in agen him"—language was'nt powerful enough to express the little gentleman's feelings here, and so he gave a most expressive and contemptuous snap of his fingers; answered by as peculiar a grunt from his companion, a fifteen-stone piece of solidity, with an acre or so of countenance, on which was legibly inscribed this simple record—that he was ever willing to hear anything anybody had got to say, but that he should reserve to himself that glorious privilege of an Englishman, of believing just as much as he liked of it, and no more. The grunt was but an echo of the expression.

"The thing is all *squared*, then, is it?" thought I, as I looked at poor Archy, who was looking at himself, and gradually fitting his neck to a bit of well-folded cambric that "the Dean" himself might have taken a notion from. Still I had too much tact to tell him what I had learned, and so on we went to business. Rumour was right on the other tack too : the line *was* a stiff one—not a merely plastered and pointed make-up, but a regular home-made rough one, with some very curious doubles—a lane that was neither good to get into or out of—and a brook about a mile from home, with very much the same kind of recommendation. Of course we weren't going to grumble; and whatever the Weavers thought, they didn't. In fact, their jockey, a good-tempered, black-whiskered, dark-visaged fellow, whom everybody seemed to know, and everybody as regularly hailed as "Tom," had a reputation for riding at anything required, while The Weaver himself was a known good-hearted one. I cannot say I troubled myself much about the other four, who, with these two, were taken some way down to fight it out, while I went into the Stand to compose my feelings, and see what I could of it.

The fame of The Weaver, or nothing else "on," had brought down some of the regular ring-men, conspicuous amongst whom was the sable-suited, sallow-faced one I saw in the coffee-room. The offensive tone was stronger than ever. I never heard a man say what he had to say in such a disagreeable voice in my life; and the defiant jarring way in which he repeated his offer to "Lay agen the grey," almost drove me wild. He didn't appear to deign to know the horse had a name on the card, though he had what we thought a very good as well as a very classic one—"Apelles" *to wit*—but round and round he went, with "I'LL LAY AGEN THE GREY!" And whenever he got a taker, which he did occasionally, out came the defiant stronger than ever, with a sort of sneering "Would you like to do it again, sir?" I was positively compelled to take his thirty to five to prevent my doing something yet more outrageous; though I felt, as he asked my name and booked the bet, that it was all "squared," and no mistake.

* * * * *

"*They are off!*" says somebody, who appears to have a peculiar pleasure in being the first to proclaim it; but it is a long way "off," and we only get a bird's-eye view now and then. There is a bit of a hitch, though, at the third fence, one of the big doubles already mentioned. White-jacket, leading, turns right away from it—*No go*, sir; and three are well away again before he jumps into it. A little more coquetting and he is out again; but white-jacket won't do here. "Well saved!" at the next fence: the little chesnut mare was on her head, but nothing worse; and round the hill they rattle, a good-looking grey horse making play, with a great slashing brown pulling hard on his quarter; three more in a cluster, and white-jacket still in the rear. We shan't see any more of them for some time; not well, indeed, till they top the hill again for the run home; while here, in the interim, the excitement becomes greater than ever. "*Three to one against anything, bar one—*" "*I'll take six to four I name the winner—*" and "I'll lay agen the grey," of course from my vindictive friend in the suit of sables.

* * * * * *

"Here they are again," sings out Sister Anne, from his corner of the Stand; and Apelles, screwed famously through an unshorn bull-fincher, comes "a stunner" for the brook. There are only three with him, but the black-whiskered hero is one of them, pulling his horse beautifully together, and certainly looking as well, or better, than anything. *Hurrah!* well jumped, by Jupiter! and Archy is over and away again—"The Weaver's down!" says everybody almost at the same moment: a less interesting gentleman is nearly out of sight in the full luxury of his cold bath; while the chesnut mare is the only other one safely landed. I hardly dare what to hope; it is barely a mile from home, and if it *is* "squared" still——

"The Grey for a Pony!" roars out somebody at my elbow in the voice of a Stentor. "The Grey wins, for a Pony.—*Done* wi' you.—Yes, I'll do it again—*Done* wi' you, sir. I'll lay odds on one."

Conceive my astonishment! it was my old enemy, the undertaker, who, with an utter disregard for all consistency of character and conduct, was now as vehemently supporting my horse as he had just previously been decrying him. But it is all the way of the world, thought

I to myself, as I moved from him to watch the race home —a pretty close one between the two, for the chesnut mare showed a turn of speed, and had been very carefully ridden all through. So close, indeed, did they finish, that when an over-excited man in spectacles, who hadn't a shilling on it, and didn't know a soul in it, asked me in much trepidation, "What had won?" I really hesitated a bit, as I stammered out I thought that my—I mean the ——

"O, 'Apples' won, safe enough," declared the gentleman in black once more, in his over-confident way; " and I loses a hundred on it, s'help me!"

He was right; "Apples" had won; and it was past ten o'clock, I'm afraid, before Archy and I reached the vicarage that night. There must have been some suspicion, too, I fancy, as to what kept us; for in addition to the Doctor asking pointedly after the health of the back-sinew, Bessy Gradus remarked, in her quiet way, at breakfast—

"What a funny term a steeple-chase is! I wonder what it is. Wasn't there one near the town, yesterday? Did you hear who won, Mr. Softun?"

She knows all about it now, though; for the degree was a good one, after all, and somehow—

But isn't this "immaterial" here?

THE FATE OF ACTÆON.

"On Monday next, the property of a gentleman without reserve," &c., &c.

Those ancients, take them one and all,
    Were certainly as queer a set
As ever made romance sing small,
    Or put a critic on the fret.
The way they laughed at every rule
    Of common good, or common sense;
The style in which they played the fool,
    "Regardless quite of all expense;"
And here 'tis worthy of remark,
    The very first to run in debt, or
Make a row, or lush, or lark,
    Were such as should have known better:
Just as in later days we see,
    In cases as to breaking lamps
The greatest—that's in pedigree—
    Are generally the greatest scamps.

Their laws too, of old, for marauder and felon,
Is another strange point just a moment to dwell on.
    If a chap did anything anyways odd,
    The fashion they had of applying the rod
    Was, instead of clapping him into quod,
    As sure as a gun to make him a *God*.

The moderns, again, have it here as well,
As witness our second parallel:—
    If a gentleman much overcome with beer
    Hits out right and left at everything near,
    And makes up a charge most uncommonly clear,
    The papers report it " the freak of a *Peer*."

In committing, then, curious sorts of crimes
    The learned alike in this agree—
That the ancients quite equalled the present times,
    As *vide* the pages of his-to-ry.
A woman or wine the common cause,
    That led to excesses so very distressing,
And sent up, amidst the greatest applause,
    The offender to beg for King Jupiter's blessing.
Yet sport, true sport—the flood and field—
    In those days had their full attractions;
And many a dandy's fate was sealed
    With " glory" in these warlike actions.
His foot had slipped, or spear had broken,
    Down bore the boar with fatal speed,
To prove, ere yet a word was spoken,
    A very horrid bore indeed.
Or the hound had turned, or horse had backed,
    And so lost the master's life or game;
For, as Neighbour Constance gives the fact,
    " You sportsmen never are to blame."

There are lots of stories of this hue,
    For which to Ovid I'd refer;
Or if his " Latin's Greek to you,"
    Consult that useful work, Lempriére.

From out the whole, p'raps none so clear-
  Ly impressed, or widely known is,
As, thanks to William Shakespeare's care,
  The one of Venus and Adonis.
Still here 'tis love, 'tis love, 'tis love,
  That spins the story round and round—
Adonis is but a "sucking dove,"
  And not the man to cap a hound.
    But luckily his fate's used up,
    And so our hungry muse may sup
      On stronger fare
      Than smile or tear,
      Or locks of hair,
      Or " duck and dear"—
  Though at the last few men would growl
  If reduced to reality—flesh and fowl.

You have seen the showman, 'midst awful din,
  Hurry his troop of strollers in;
    While bell and gong
    Assure the throng
"They're really just a going to begin."
You have seen in the kennel the gallant pack,
When there wasn't the need of a whip to crack,
To keep the well-trained lot of 'em back,
  As, one by one, they were drafted out:
You have seen the huntsman fix his eyes
On Nonplus, unequalled for form and size;
You at such a hound, too, expressed your surprise—
  Though of hounds you know little about.

I am the showman in the midst of the din,
Hurrying my strolling facts all in;
  While line by line,
  You may well divine,
I'm really just a going to begin.
 My second simile's yet more clear—
 "Get back Venus; what do you do here?
 Hie! *sus*—ACTÆON! here boy, here."
Like a well-bred dog he hears my call—
The curtain rises, and—attention all.

Once on a time—when time was young,
And his chronicles either said or sung,
But seldom printed—there dwelt in Thrace,
Or just on the borders of some such place,
A gentleman greatly attached to the chase.
This term, though, "attached," is rather conventional,
And if, in this place, not permitted to mention all
The items and likings that led to the phrase,
Being thus introduced, I'll still, "if you plaze,"
Take a moment or two to make out an invoice
Of a few leading points in the man of my choice.
And first—*lucus a non*—I'll just show you what
The gentleman was, by what he was not;
A course that may sound not a little indicative
"Of proving," as counsel would tell us, "a negative."

He wasn't a satin-tyed sweet-scented swell,
A London-built buck for a Leamington belle;
Nor did he make hunting for gaming the net,
To be wound up with cards, or to bring on a bet;
He wasn't a varmint, 'cute, pattern-slang knave,
Whose virtue was linen as clean as his shave—

Who nicked in a run, as he nicked on " the main,"
To sell man or horse, if it were but his gain.
In short, to adopt Serjeant Goulbourn's expression,
The chase was " the pleasure, and not the profession"
Of my hero, whose taste ne'er to dealing descended,
Whose morning's delight with " the box " never ended,
Nor " the leg" with the glad tally-ho ever blended.
His passion too pure—and thanked be the gods!—
To class him with city clerks settling the odds—
Verbum sap, from his fellows a man you may ken,
His fellows were sportsmen, and not sporting men.

    And here, as my muse is going to excess,
    Your pardon I crave, while I slightly digress,
        To keep her from the greater riot;
    Just as from the cover a fretful steed
    Is rattled up the adjoining mead,
        To tone his fire and get him quiet;
    Soh—now then, off we send the rusher
    Up, what the lads would call a " brusher."

Come, gent; thy tastes for once I'll brook;
Come, bearded count, with thy loathsome look;
Come, methodist parson, with nasal whine;
Come, Jew, with thy rings and chains so fine—
Come, snob, come tailor, come one, come all,
Every nod I'll honour, return each call,
If penance so heavy but save me can
From the sportsman's bane—the sporting man.

Let me jostle the crowd upon Ludgate's hill,
To see aldermen riding to " Eat-and-swill;"

Or, oppressed with shop-boys, heat, and spleen,
In a half-price pit let me watch the scene;
Or, as usher, in vain endeavour to rule
The imps at a thriving " Commercial School ;"
Or swallow the speeches, meats, and creed,
Brought out at a grand political feed—
Come, what you will, anywhere and when,
But a sportman's *trade* with sporting men.

To resume—friend Actæon, a plain country squire,
With a love for the rural that nothing could tire;
With a nice little income, in money paid down,
Quite enough for a man not "a man about town;"
Hung out in a cottage, snug, cosy, and neat,
In the market, no doubt, they would call it "a seat;"
A cottage content to sport some such a label
As, "a good eight-room house, with a sixteen-stall stable."
Here he shot, hunted, fished, taking season for season,
But ne'er marking his game at a price beyond reason ;
Made his purse fit his pleasures, his pleasures his purse,
Feared no bills overdue, need no property "nurse;"
And in short managed all on that capital plan,
With his bankers "a safe," with the sex "a sweet man."
Aye! despite dogs and horses, crowds of mothers and daughters,
Looked at Tally-ho Lodge as "uncommon nice" quarters.
Hinted, joking *of course*, with an eye slightly slanting,
There was *one* piece of furniture sadly yet wanting—
And then Jane played the chorus, Emmy sang "Chanticleer,"
Or Fan larked her pony—"such a sweet little dear;"

G

While old mother Gracch—something had always "just
    been" to him,
To call, or invite, or—to stick Susan into him.

Alas! that pride should have a fall;
Alas! that the envy of 'em all,
So proof to all their traps and crosses,
Should yield still more to dogs and "hosses;"
Or, as Glaucopis set the case,
"What a pity he's so much attached to the chase."

Kean's life has started many an actor;
Jack Sheppard's, many a malefactor;
Childe Harold Byron's, fierce men-haters;
Cook's voyages, fresh navigators;
The hunting tours "took" e'en with Schneiders,
And writing of 'em made "Crack Riders;"
Old Izaak's lines have wetted many a line,
And jocks been formed from "Genius Genuine."
Our instance, though, is yet more classic a
One—'tis the *Notitia Venatica*—
A work that a vast deal of merit has,
And proves the saw, "*in Vyner Veritas.*"
Its point, however, is simply this,
That to arrive at perfect bliss
In the true pleasure of the chase,
You mustn't take a second place;
But having somehow got the knack,
Keep, hunt, and *feed* yourself the pack,
Showing an M.F.H. to be,
The happiest man that "you shall see:"

THE FATE OF ACTÆON.

Actæon read it.—
*   *   *   *   *

Of all the many means and ways
  That lead a man to proper glory,
How few so soon shall "reach the case,"
  Like that great art—to tell a story;
The Attic salt, the fit expression,
  The rhythm neat—if told in song—
And then that crowning nice discretion
  That makes the story not *too long*.
Discretion! dear, sweet, brown-bread saint!
  Thou guardian of our love and life;
Who keeps the maiden "fresh as paint"
  'Till fairly owned and known a wife;
Who hedges off the leg's grand "pot,"
  And makes his book to smell of mint;
Who marks the actor, stays the sot,
  And bows the poet into print—
Discretion! unknown wondrous maid!
  Stretch forth a hand ere yet too late,
For one who now first asks your aid,
  And save him from his hero's fate!

    That Fate, the text that brims our cup,
      Is settled in a "summing up."

With smallish means what great effrontery,
Notes him who dares to hunt a country—
Hounds, horses, servants, open house,
Earth-stoppers, keepers—"safe" to chouse—

---

* We have his copy, a very curious black letter one, of the original edition, which a Great Great ancestor of our own bought at the sale in a lot with some couples and blacking bottles.

Balls, banquets, Gunter, Jullien down,
With hosts of *artistes* straight from town;
Donations, plates for hunters' stakes,
With plenty more in " ducks and drakes;"
Which will, of course, be paid off, one and all,
By " the subscription "—*query*, nominal?

Actæon stood it just three years,
And then—o'ercome with costs and cares,
And duns and bums, and foxes few,
" Short-answering" slaves with wages due,
And " Fields" that looked uncommon blue—
At eve, when o'er a poor day's sport,
And o'er as poor a glass of port
(For out, alas! " the favourite sort "),
Owned to himself the soft delusion,
And, having come to this conclusion,
Laid down his horn with half a curse,
Hung up his whip, pulled off his spurs,
Then, like a cock, his feathers moulted,
Packed up his saddle-bags and—*bolted.*

Farther than this the fable goes,
And in its version boldly shows,
How with a cry so full and grim,
The hounds set to and hunted him,
Ran him at length from scent to view,
And " broke him up" with small to do;
Yet, though the Musters* case is clear,
The other can't pass muster here.

---

* The well known anecdote of Mr. Musters and his hounds, as see the *Notitia*.

THE FATE OF ACTÆON.

The eating up a man is common
Enough, by horse, or hound, or woman;
Or even in some situations,
By his own friends and dear relations;
But still the phrase the fact transgresses,
When in such terms "a smash" expressed is—
Enough to prove on what allegory
The ancients pitched so strong a story.

Be as it may—quite eaten up,
  Or only out of house and home
By friends who stop to dine and sup,
  Still to this point at last we come:—
Do what you will—fight, drink, or play,
  Your fortune somehow to get through;
Spend it the most immoral way,
  There always is a moral too.

When in the next new comedy
  The scampish character comes on,
With swaggering air and manner free,
  That on the stage must pass for *ton*;
When the father gives his glad consent
  For Scamp to take Sophia in marriage,
And tells to his friend the great event,
  And how the suitor keeps his carriage:
Mark, then, that friend with wary eye,
  Give out this well worn, honoured whim—
"Sir David, hark, 'twixt you and I,
  The carriage 'tis that's keeping him."

So gentlemen all, with incomes but small,
Who don't want to fall, or go to the wall,

But weather a squall, and keep up the ball;
Attend to my lay, and mind what I say,
As to making your play for *more* than a day,
And being able to pay your share and your way.
If twice out a week with the pack within hail,
And sport in proportion supposed to be shown,
Finds you still rather prone to grumble and rail,
And, like Nelson, you want "a Gazette of your own;"
With subscriptions *collected*,
And kennels erected,
With a nerve to ride screws,
"On the fast and the loose,"
And people that really come out for the fun;
With lodgings got cheap,
Just to breakfast and sleep;
Then a heart for your sport,
And on something this sort
Of plan *the thing has been, and is to be, done.*

And now, as the poet sighs adieu,
Remember well his counsel true,
And with Actæon's fate in view,
If you keep hounds—let hounds keep you.

A COPER'S CONFESSION.

"I think, Tester, I've been a very tolerable master to you."
"Very tolerable indeed, Sir."　　　　　　　　　Old Play.

There are few men, I feel bound to say, who can have a greater regard for thorough independency of character than myself; and yet it has been my constant aim through life to act up to that beautiful old English axiom which so touchingly develops itself in this simple inquiry —"What *is* the use of having a friend if you *don't* make use of him?"

By this candid avowal, I would not wish it to be understood that I treat my round of acquaintance just as I should their pheasants and hares—by taking one single shot at, and then have done with them. Far from it. I flatter myself I am too good a judge to commit so monstrous an outrage on their good fellowship or my own good feeling. I would never, for example, gammon a man, with a civil smile and insinuating address, into standing security for any of my little road-side liabilities; never wish him to be guilty of perjury in testifying to the morality of my character or the sobriety of my conduct; and would as soon think of asking him to lend me his wife for three weeks as his name for three months. No, no; the very nature of these sort of things has, I am convinced, let them turn out how they will, a direct tendency to knocking your name off "the free list;" and consequently I have generally confined my operations to the loan of last numbers of magazines, clean shirts, opera-glasses, half-crowns, umbrellas, and such like trifles, which, as a matter of course, no gentleman is ever expected to recollect or return—without it suits his convenience so to do.

Still, any allusion to one grand item I have purposely omitted in the above enumeration—one particularly adapted to my present purpose, and one which, from the experience and success I have enjoyed in pursuing it, I am very much inclined to consider as my own peculiar property. It consists in nothing more or less than an innate and high ability for *borrowing horses*. Egad! the very mention of my secret in such plain language nearly stays me from proceeding; for the plan hitherto has been so systematically subtle as to have almost at last deceived its author himself. Here, by the bye, I would warn the very open-hearted, unsuspecting auditor from supposing my attacks could come in any such shape as the following: "My dear Williams—got the young ones home for the holidays—like to give 'em a treat—Hampton Court—offer of neighbour's four wheel—venture to hint—your beautiful brown pony—all admire so much —loath to disappoint the ladies—yours ever and ever, &c., &c." And "dear Williams," picturing to himself his "beautiful brown pony" toiling through town in the heat of a July noonday sun, with his head loose, and Ma and Pa, and Ben and the baby, in front; and Jennie and Annie, and aunt Mary and Mr. M'Carthy, the medical student, and a rabbit pie, and a fillet of veal, and a Yorkshire ham, and a rhubarb tart, and a bottle of salad, behind—returns in answer either "his compliments, and he's very sorry to say he shall want the pony every day for the next six months; or, if he has anything like the heart and humour of ourselves, encloses a post-office order for fifteen shillings!

What otherwise should be expected from such "an impudent attempt at robbery?" And then just compare it with my perfect, actually *obliging*, style of going to work. I never wanted *to borrow a horse*, but I persuaded his owner I wanted to *buy him*. And the troops I have taken horse exercise on at these terms! and the provoking little defects which prevented my purchasing—heads a *leetle* too long, or tails too short—nice hack, but wouldn't suit me, as he'd not been in harness—or a clever animal, certainly, but a heavy goer, had him in a minute if he hadn't been in harness—too big, too small, too fat, too sluggish, too leggy, too punchy. By Jupiter! if I had only bought one in a hundred of the horses I've tried, Mr. Collins must long since have hid his diminished head, and the lower end of Oxford-street have erected a monument to my memory.

But few pursuits—I may not say pleasures—are without their drawbacks, and a plain statement of one of the heaviest and most unavoidable I ever experienced may tend to the edification of any who feel inclined to adopt my profession.

The winter before last found me breaking into February with far from the feeling of having had *enough* of the hunting season. To be sure, I had three days with the Queen on a thorough-bred, sky-scraping tit, which a sucking barrister was very anxious to get out of, and which I *fancied* at first I rather liked; had condemned again a couple of machiners for an ex-Jobmaster, after trying their merits with the Surrey—one because he couldn't jump, the other because he wouldn't try; and had been *persuaded* also to feel the mouth of a third-rate steeple-chaser in a scurry with the Hertfordshire, during which his owner evinced a very laudable, but I need scarcely add, unavailable ambition, to stick "Young Vivian" into me. Well, Christmas was passed, and I saw nothing for it, but a line to a friend in a far county explaining my want of horse, price not over a hundred, and age not under six; this, as I expected, produced an invitation, and away I went without further notice to try his stud and his board. The first morning after my arrival was chosen for the first taste of the string; but in which my host could not accompany me, being nailed for a special jury cause at the assizes, on the usual conditions of gaining a guinea if he did go, and losing ten if he did not. Previous, however, to setting forth, he gave me full particulars of the nag I was about to cross: age rising eight, or, by the book, just that age; figure, my maximum—eighty-five guineas, in fact, having already been offered by an officer quartered in the neighbourhood; and character as to pace, fencing, and temper, as near perfection as possible. One thing only in the way of command was strongly impressed upon me—that whether I liked my horse or not, I was to *go along with him*, for the captain was still on the nibble, and one decisive day's work might hook him outright. "In short, sir," concluded my friend, "the grey, I know, as Sir Charles Bunbury said, will do *his* duty if you do *yours*, and consequently I shan't hear of any excuse. Bring home a lame horse if you must, but I can't admit of a lame story." And with that he started to find a verdict, and I a fox.

The grey certainly, as far as appearances went, was

worthy all that could be said of him; and in the three-mile ride to the meet I had some opportunity of proving his more important accomplishments. I dropped my hand, gave him his head, and away he walked with an ease and confidence that quickly imparted itself to his rider: then I jogged him into a trot that finished as sure and as safe as a Welsh pony's; while, last of all, I sent him at three parts speed up a green bite by the road-side, from which I confess I pulled him up in no little chagrin, not to say dissatisfaction: he went *so* oily and well—playing with the plain snaffle in his mouth, arching his neck, and bending to the hand in a manner truly delightful.

"Egad!" said I, "if Blue Peter (so they called him) only turns out half as well as he promises, I'm fixed at once; for where the deuce shall I ever find a fault or a reason to give the Squire for *not* buying him?"

But let me get to the cover-side—a large wood, from eighty to a hundred and twenty acres in extent, with plenty of good lying, and, from its situation in the heart of an otherwise open country, worth its length in gold to the man who hunted it. A fox, three or four indeed, were soon a-foot, but, despite plenty of rattling about from one side to another, not much inclined to break; seeming to think that if there was any thing like the scent out there was *in* cover, it could not be much use their having a run for it. Not knowing a yard of my ground, the cover being large and the wind strong, I thought it advisable to keep as near as I could to the pack, and for nearly two hours continued wriggling and twisting up and down the awfully heavy rides, in, I am sorry to say, a good deal of that slack rein, rough-riderish, hard-hearted manner, which men will occasionally adopt with horses they either don't own or deserve. During this terribly prolonged prologue, however, an opportunity was afforded me of looking over the field; and I and the soldier gradually deciphered each other. He was a six foot, fine made fellow, though with rather a ferretish face—large white moustache, and small red eye—mounted on a neat little chesnut mare, certainly not more than fourteen three, which, with his own long shanks, gave the pair a very jack-a-dandyish appearance. His companion—the hero or crack man of the hunt—was the only other person I had any particular cause to notice: a thin, light-complexioned young man, in highly polished jack-boots, with an eye-glass stuck in his hat, and a sneering sort of smile on his face; unquestionably under ten stone, but riding a blood bay stallion up to at least fourteen. Now, no sooner was a fox forced to fly—an event which at length did come to pass—than I found this brace of swells had made a dead set at the stranger: every time he made a move, it was "eyes right" on him, though for some time without any decided advantage on either side. I had followed King Herod (the stallion) over a couple of high new gates, shown him the way at a good drain with a bad take-off, and rather excelled the military man in three or four of his own hop, step, and a jump, or on and off fences, when a low holly-hedge, with a very long drop, which experience enabled them to avoid, struck the balance against me: poor Peter, in sheer surprise, came on his head, and I went over it—a piece of agility which I at once saw had the effect of curling the captain's hair-lip, and adding considerably to the broad grin of the hard-riding skeleton. All this put my blood up; but as soon as ever I got righted again, I luckily had a chance for putting *them* down: the hounds, running like mad, had crossed a lane, the only exit from which was as nasty a stile as ever I came across in my life: a single stone slab, about four feet high, looking ominously like a gravestone, stuck upon rising ground, with two cruelly placed stepping-stones before you reached it, and a cart-load or so more lying loose around them—a very nice, pleasing impediment, no doubt, to hand a young *lady* over, but a mightily different affair when you attempted the same piece of politeness with a young *horse*. Well, King Herod was a hard-pulling, hot-headed beggar, that rushed at everything he attempted; so the eye-glass, with very excellent discretion, was brought into service for something more inviting. The captain, too, was not in any vast hurry, when at that moment—I do believe they had forgotten me—I touched the crack on one of his jack-boots with the handle of my whip, tipped him a civil and cool " By your leave, Sir," and trotted Blue Peter up to it. He picked his way like a cat, measured his ground to an inch, and hopped over with a finished grace that even now makes my heart beat to think of it. Yet, alas for the force of example! before I could turn my head the bay stallion had chested it in one of his wild charges, and rolled over with a *smash* that sent the rest of the field down the lane as hard as they could pelt.

Revenge is a very vile passion, I allow, the indulgence in which is only admitted by bravos and barbarians, yet I think just then I had the happy man's shirt in my possession.

* * * * *

It is extraordinary, but no man yet, I believe, was ever found with sufficient candour to acknowledge the advantages of a check ; at any rate it was not exactly with a blessing that I saw the hounds hang fire round some farm buildings—of a truth I was not at all in the best of humours, for I was the only man fairly up, had been carried magnificently; and *ergo* there was that purchasing incubus still heavy on me, though in intent wonderfully altered.

"My income was not large," I reasoned; "the season was nearly over—a hundred guineas was a great deal of money—and what would my mother say if she heard of it? But, then a hundred for *such* a horse! *pshaw!* Quibbler as I was, what excuse could I make to MYSELF if I *didn't have him?*"

After a ten minutes' lull, during which some half-dozen reappeared, including the King Herod firm, very strongly lithographed, the steed with plenty of skin-deep evidence of his mishap, and his pilot with the loss of the smile and the eye-glass, a head whip—somehow or other head whips, as far as horsemanship goes, always are the head of the establishment—set us going again.

To follow the fortunes of this second heat in any great detail would, I fear, verge upon the tedious; sufficient be it, then, to say, that with, if anything, an increasing pace, I still "followed the hounds;" beginning with a terribly stiff rail out of the rick-yard; that the whip followed *me* as well as he could; and that the rest nicked, crept, crawled, and looked on until we arrived at one of those plain-speaking, anti-humbugging contrivances, a brook. *A brook*, be it understood: not one of those ditch-water affairs we hear so much about after dinner, but a real brook, or a river if you like, twenty feet full in the only practicable place, and deep enough to float a frigate. Well, what with skilful manœuvring and the fortune of war, the *militaire*, who exhibited, I must say, a vast deal more of Mac-Adamised mud than proper glory about his equipment, got the first offer at it, and worked away with his long legs in a desperate energy, that certainly meant mischief on his part; but this was the full extent of it—there was none in his little mare, who beat to a standstill, never even made an effort, but tumbled, utterly powerless, into the middle, and was out of sight in an instant; while just as the gallant Captain came sputtering and puffing to the top again, *I went slap*—" clean and clever," *over his head!*

" By the powers!" I exclaimed, in an ecstacy, as I rammed in the spurs and ran up to the very sterns of the pack—" By the powers, friend Peter, but you're *mine*, now and for ever!"

* * * * *

How long or how far we had been running were matters on which I could give but a very vague opinion; my total ignorance of the country preventing any decent estimate of the one, and the excitement I was labouring under, of the other. Whether, again, the fox would ever evince any signs of sinking appeared equally dubious. But from these considerations my attention was quickly taken in another quarter. To my great astonishment, I really began to fancy I was getting a peep at, what Mr. Green would call, " the left-hand" side of my horse: he hit an oak-stile I put him at, with every leg he had to his body, only just saving himself from further effects in a listless, Devil-me-care way, that spoke infinite danger; then he followed this up by refusing, three times in succession, so unequivocally and determinedly, that I felt fain to give in to him. And when, thanks to a burning scent, the pack made one of those beautifully sudden and simultaneous turns right across the point I was steering for, and compelled me to pull him into a trot, he hung so heavy on my hand, and went in such a mechanical, deadly-lively manner, that I was all but convinced I had been judging too hastily :—uncertain at timber, a resolute refuser, want of bottom, and a bad mouth.

"Come, come, Peter, my boy!" said I, clapping to him again, on entering one of those doomed domains of the public, an open common—"Come, come, it will never do to go and rub out all the fine things we have been performing to-day, in this fashion!" For a few strides he answered me gallantly enough; but the roads, crossroads, diggings for turf, and deep cart ruts, soon brought us to the trot again; in which he at length made a mistake, and, after tottering forward for a few yards, fell, without caring to recover himself, heavily on his side. I was on my legs in an instant, and catching short hold of his bridle, endeavoured, but in vain, to rouse him to a like position. Directly I loosened the rein, his head dropped perfectly inanimate, and, with a deep groan, or rather sigh, he stretched himself out in a way that at once stopt me from any further attempt."

"He's dead beat, sure enough," thought I aloud, after looking at him for a minute or so in silence.

"Hur's *dead* enough any-hows," responded a countryman at my shoulder; who seemed, like one of the armed men of old, to have risen from the earth at a moment's notice. "Hur's *dead* enough anyhow, I reckon."

"Good heavens! d'ye think so?"

"No, I don't; I be sure on't."

He was! and then all the events of the day at once came across me: the two or three hours' work in the sticky rides of the cover, the subsequently terrific pace and distance we had travelled, the indisputable style in which I had beaten every thing else out of sight, and the courage and readiness with which my poor horse *did* go as long as he *could* go, all rose to reproach me. Under any circumstances, my case was unpleasant in the extreme; but what renders it still more so was the unpalatable truth that *would* force itself upon me—the horse wasn't *mine!*

What followed I need not dilate upon. I had found out his failing—he wasn't *immortal*. Let me merely add that, on my way back, I fully sympathized with that unhappy gentleman who, tradition reports, once advertised for "an agreeable companion in a post-chaise." I am afraid indeed just now to name the sum I would have given for any one of any kind—the amiable man who employs his "Kentish fire" in shooting the foxes, or the right reverend gentleman who runs his muck against the race-week providing they promised to rigmarole incessantly on the road, should not have been refused a seat by my side. My friend, who, on first seeing me, imagined I had sold his favourite, an idea on which I was quickly compelled to *sell* him, bore it like an Englishman or a Spartan woman, only remarking on my concluding, "He died, Sir, the death of a hero, for he died on the field." Offering consolation at such times is always a ticklish affair: some vulgar-minded men would tender it in a pecuniary sense; but the sufferer, with his mind harassed quite enough already, is very apt to take any such intent as an insult, and I am sure my good tact and consideration will be properly appreciated when I declare I did *not*.

That night I went to bed with the full determination of never trying another horse without I actually wanted one; but maybe the reader has heard the story of "the Jolly

Companion" who, on meeting a fellow-spirit at the cover side, inquired when he was drunk last? To which the other seriously replied that he had left off drinking; and, when pressed again as to how long, ingenuously answered ever since three o'clock that morning. This much resembles my vow; the next day but one I threw my leg over a brown mare, which in a sharp thing of five-and-twenty minutes, went nearly as well as the departed Peter: she had, however, a trick of pricking her ears and fixing her eye while hounds were running in cover, that to me looked very like vice, and I consequently was reluctantly forced to decline her. On that evening, too, I bade my friend adieu, returning to town to try a wall-eyed Augur filly, which Harboro' Magna Green wrote me word was "the very thing for me;" a confident assurance which in my own mind I felt much inclined to doubt.

By the way, as I hear there is another "Blue Peter" about, I must put in a claim to the original title for poor Peter: by which, indeed, he stands registered in the *Stud Book*, for he was as thorough-bred as a Spanish Don or Cheshire Pile.

FULWAR CRAVEN:

"A BIT OF A CHARACTER."

"Fulwar Craven," as with something more than a contempt for the conventional *Mr.* he insisted on being called, was a bit of a character it was hard to lose. There was an eccentricity about the man that was all his own. It was in obedience neither to any passing whim of fashion nor the "fancy" that he chose to be odd and remarkable —and remarkable he always was. He was an original, no doubt, in a day when there were more of the sort than there are in our own dull and decorous times; but even then, he ever stood out from amongst his fellows. Try him by the severest of tests. Take him at Ascot in, perhaps, the very prime of its history, as that glorious procession was seen rising the New Mile—when youth and beauty, wealth and taste, rank and splendour, did all they could to enchant one. When D'Orsay the Magnificent displayed his wristbands, threw back his light overcoat, and rejoiced in the enormous spread of his blue satin stock, just as a peacock might in the full effulgence of his plumage. When good Sir Gilbert, always a bit of a buck in his way, gave us a thorough "study" of the Old English Gentleman, with the silver buttons on his coat, the silver cord to the knees of his breeches, the one or two smart under-waistcoats, and the immaculate white cravat. When "the Assassin," with all the daring courage of youth and genius, started such a collar for a coat as set the beef-eating, short-necked yeomen of Berks half wild with envy and despair of imitation. When her pretty little ladyship treated you to a glimpse of her pretty little foot, and an inch or so of ankle that the classic sandal clung so lovingly around. When the Marchioness Maria raised her glass and waved her long ringlets in the summer breeze, to the admiration of all beholders, but evidently to none more so than the dark dandy at her elbow. When the Master of the Buckhounds proclaimed himself, as he passed you, by the silver emblem of his order; and Davis seeming, as it were, to bear the very impress of royalty about him, turned the head of his chesnut thorough-bred, and rode back side-by-side with Robinson, who has just saddled for the Swinley. And in the midst of all these—the royal liveries, the Windsor uniforms, the gauzy dresses, the smart bonnets, and the bright eyes flashing from out of them—from the very horse you are backing even, you turn for another look at that strange-looking man. What a slang, defiant, and yet somehow thorough sportsman's air there is about him! What a deal of devil in his eye, and a life's story, surely, in his very walk and bearing! The careless cock of his battered white hat is of itself all "character," supported, as this is, by the wisp tie of his crimson bandana, the half-open striped waistcoat, and the loose cut of his brass-buttoned brown coat, with another fogle flying from the pocket of it. Then his drab breeches and gaiters are almost equally decisive, even if not emphasised, as they are, by the latter being studiously pulled down at the back, to show some inches of a pink silk stocking. Mark, again, the big brooch in his shirt, the purple jacket in his hand, and the roving glance as he goes. "He's a curiosity," says your country friend with a half smile—"and yet he is somebody." Observe with what profound court the great Jerry himself greets him! What a flourish he gives the cocked hat in the elaboration of his salute! And how discreet, even in his impudence, he asks so respectfully, "Shall I put my trifle on the filly, Mr. Craven?" He has let out our secret, you see, though the trainer comes up with a touch of the hat almost at the moment. *That is* Fulwar Craven—

" So prime, so flash, so nutty, and so knowing"—

the owner of Deception and Longwaist, the swell ex-Captain Craven, the game evergreen, as ready still as any of you for a bout, a lark, or a drink—

" Who loves not woman, wine, and song,
Lives a fool's life his whole life long."

Ah! that rural beauty in the straw bonnet has driven "I-wish-you-may-get it" and the handicap clean out of his head already—only to be recovered, Mr. Treen, by the black-eyed Gipsy, who will "patter" him to his heart's content, and wish him luck in a lingo that it is perhaps quite as well no one else knows a word of.

With all that innate taste for rural pursuits and pastimes which most country gentlemen inherit with their estates, it is still as a Turfite that Fulwar Craven will be remembered. He hunted occasionally, and even at one period had a pack of harriers of his own. He was a good shot, and fond of it, but never a heavy game preserver; while the famous trout-fishing on his Chilton property early initiated him into the nice art and mystery of throwing a fly. But with a commission in the *First Royals*, our " dashing" youngster, as they called them in those times, soon rose to higher game than filling a creel or hunting the hare. A turn for racing was then almost as prominent amongst the follies of the day as it is still; and in 1807, "— Craven, Esq.," ran his first horse, Pic-nic, at Reading. By the next season, he was a subscriber to the *Calendar*, and drew first blood at so imposing a place as Newmarket, where he won his maiden race, a match, with the significantly titled " Fly by Night;" and Charles Goodison, a brother of the more famous Tom, as his first jockey. Bantam, by Gohanna, was another favourite and a better nag; while he was fond enough of Jannette to think he could win the Oaks with her. This was in 1810, and the Captain consoled himself for the disappointment by his marriage in the same year; and for a long period his passion for the turf was put into abeyance. Even, indeed, as a racing man his orbit was eccentric, and for ten or twelve years he had not a horse in work; but in '24 he came to the post again in far greater form than ever. That very *clever* man, John Dilly, of Littleton, who added a touch of the saint to his other eminent qualifications, was engaged to train, and the elegant Sam Day, then in his very zenith as a jockey, took the purple jacket and orange cap into his keeping. They brought half-a-dozen out during the season, and amongst them a couple of three-year-olds, purchased of Forth, the trainer. With one of these Mr. Craven again believed he could win the Oaks, and amongst his other great friends he got some of the blood Royal to back her. But the Duke of Gloucester met him only with a pleasant smile and a half shake of the head when it was over—" Well, Craven, you see we are all ruined by this fine Miss Jigg of yours!" The Whalebone colt turned out far better. He was christened "Longwaist," and led off well by winning what was then the great race of that part of the country, the Gloucestershire Stakes at Cheltenham. He followed this up with other good things both during that and the next year. In the latter, in fact, he came out a really great horse, carrying off the Craven and Oatlands at Newmarket, with the gold Cups—and they were gold cups in those times—at Winchester, Cheltenham, Oxford, Burderop, and Warwick. Longwaist also figured, though unsuccessfully, in two yet more memorable races—for the Cups at Ascot and at Doncaster. In the first of these his opponent was Bizarre, ridden by Arnull, while Robinson was on Longwaist. A horse called Streatham was started merely to make play for Lord George Cavendish; but Boyce, who was on him, forced the running so much that at the last turn he seemed to have the two cracks both safe, and sang out that he was winning! They managed to catch him, however, and a terribly severe and tiring race finished in favour of Bizarre. At Doncaster—it was in Memnon's Leger year—the set-to between Sam Day on Mr. Craven's horse, and George Nelson on Lottery, with Cedric, Figaro, and others behind them, was said to have been one of the most magnificent ever seen; but again the decree was half a neck against Longwaist. Still the performance was good enough to confirm his repute as a race-horse; and on the strength of it, the renowned John Mytton, of Halston, gave three thousand guineas for him. He ran a good stout horse for two or three years after this; but Mr. Craven himself stuck to it that "Longwaist was not within seven pounds as good a one as the public thought him." He was, though, a neat one to look at; long and low, standing not above fifteen-two, with a pleasant Whalebone head, and altogether of just the stamp of a wearing Cup horse. Perhaps the best, and certainly the most characteristic picture Ben Marshall ever finished was the Littleton group, as they were caught on Newmarket Heath. The sweet-tempered Sam Day sits on his snaffle-bridle, short-tailed, useful-looking nag, in that easy "home" fashion that no jockey ever sat in a picture, before or since. Then, at his head stands the sagacious Mr. Dilly, reading the list over to Captain Craven, and calculating what Lionel Lincoln can do with them at the distance. We recollect the first time we saw the print, for there was one published in the *Old Sporting Magazine*, was in Beau Shackell's sanctum in Oxford-street; and we write with one, shamefully used and soiled, before us.

There were other good performers in the Littleton troop, and amongst them Triumph, by Fyldener, that won the Cup at Abingdon, and the Oxfordshire and Leamington Stakes, all in the year. This was in 1825, when Fulwar Craven really ought to have won the race he seemed to have set his heart on—the Oaks at Epsom. There is no question but his mare Pastime was a long way the best of those that started for it; but she went lame to the post, and even then was only beaten by the finest piece of jockeyship that we have upon record. It is no discredit to say that Sam Day was out-ridden by Chifney on the plater Wings, or that the neck he won by was to none a greater surprise than to the old General himself. Another season or so saw our hero once more off the Turf. In 1827, he had only El Dorado; but with him he again carried off the Gloucestershire against Isaac Sadler's old Jocko, Isaac Day's as well-known Liston, Dr.

Faustus, and that useful class of horse. There were a good many of them whose names still live going at that era, when Mr. Pryse Pryse had Dr. Eady, and Squire West, of Alscott, Claude Loraine ; while John Mytton was teasing them with the game, everlasting Euphrates, and old Ynysymaengwyn bothering the legs and lads at a bit of pronunciation. The Squire of Chilton, however, was once more cutting it. He had only a plater left in '28, and for the next ten years there must have been some new love afloat, for beyond an entry for a hunter's stake or so, the purple and orange was seldom seen. He and Dilly did not part good friends, and a fit of disgust might have taken the keenness off his appetite.

Still he is not " dr" after all, but comes again like a good one for the third and last heat. Treen now undertakes, not only to train, but ride for him, and Isaac Sadler furnishes some of the material to work upon. In 1838, when they "ring up" once more, there is Barnacles (another winner of the Gloucestershire stake), I-wish-you-may-get-it, Carew, Doncaster, and a two-year-old Defence filly.

" Have you anything worth backing here, Craven?" is the hearty hail of an old friend, who chances to spy him from the coach-box at Beckhampton.

" Yes, I have," is the decisive answer.

" And what is it?"

" Well, a filly I am going to win the Oaks with."

The Squire was as good as his word, too ; while he might have been better, had not Treen made that fatal and too common mistake with all young jockeys, of coming clean away from his horses—a tack that never has and never will tell over Epsom. And so it fell out, that the high-actioned, round-going outsider, Bloomsbury, outwitted the lady-like Deception for the Derby, and to Blink Bonny was left the fame of breaking through the Eleanor spell. With "honest John" on her, Deception won the Oaks as she pleased, and thus at length Mr. Craven's great ambition was gratified. It is only right to say that he himself found no fault with the way in which she was ridden for the Derby; and, as he declared at the time, "I only put John Day up to satisfy the public." The Oaks filly went on to both Stockbridge and Goodwood, with only further favour; but, despite such signal success, her owner was again declining. In 1840, he had only her and Benedetta, with which he won the Hopeful, in work; and in 1842 his career closed with a couple of platers, whose names were highly emblematic of the man and his tastes just at that period. They were "Don't-say-No!" and the still more slangy "That's-the time-o'Day!"

Like many more gentlemen who have made a noise in the Ring, Fulwar Craven was little hurt by what he did on the Turf. He was a tolerably keen bettor at times, but, with all his "flash," in reality a careful man. It is true, he sold the Chilton estate, but he sold it well to Mr. Popham, and only in order to purchase the Brockhampton property, which he looked on more as the family place, and where, we believe, his father, the reverend John Craven, and his mother, were buried. Despite the disadvantage to which Mr. Fulwar Craven showed himself, he had many redeeming qualities. He was a thorough gentleman when he cared to throw off the part he had taken to, had naturally good abilities, and was a very fair scholar. He is spoken yet more highly of in his own neighbourhood as an excellent magistrate and a good landlord. Nothing delighted him more than a day's rabbit-shooting amongst his tenantry, with, of course, a jollification afterwards; and for many years he was a regular attendant at Hungerford Market in Berkshire, where they still tell some quaint stories of all he said and did. However, for the seven or eight last years of his life he had become more and more retired in his habits, and long before he died the evergreen had fairly faded out. About the last we ever saw of him in public was when, some summers since, he was wont to sit on a good-looking bay mare at the top of Rotten-row—still, even in the full flow of that high tide, as much a man of mark as ever. But, *eheu! quantum mutatus ab illo Hectore*, who, as Captain Craven, of the Royals, curvetted down the line on his stallion charger—or even how altered, in a few short years from "the thorough varmint and the real swell," who "stood Sam" for everybody in the booth, and got up a shindy, as a moral duty he owed to himself! Let us try and sketch him once again, as he sits under the shade of the Achilles, with scarcely a man of his own day left to greet him. There is the white hat, and the brown brass-buttoned coat still, and, above all, the great gold-enamelled horse and jockey brooches in his shirt—the one a memorial of Longwaist, and the other of the Oaks filly. The kerseys, though, are gone, and in their place are a pair of short, broad, banjo-pattern plaid trowsers, and drab half-gaiters. He is yet a "character," and the well-dressed mob still stare and whisper as they pass, "That's Fulwar Craven." But it is only the wreck of him. Stay a minute, and remember how all the dare-devil audacious look of that dark eye has died away. Watch the nervous, almost imbecile play about the once full, firm, and decisive mouth. See how the hair-colour has run off from that poor remnant of whisker on to his shrunken cheek. Take heed of this, ye knowing youngsters, as you swagger by in all the pride of health and manhood, with a laugh on your lips at "the old swell." Bear in mind what he was, and what you will be. Think of the pace he has gone, and how, that in his prime there was hardly one of you could have lived alongside of him!

THE GREAT HANDICAP RACE.

(FROM THE FURTHER EXPERIENCES OF A. SOFTUN, ESQ.)

"WELL, but that's very odd, Alfred. You say he *could* have won the race; and yet he didn't!".

"He was 'nobbled,' my dear."

"He was *what?*"

"Oh!—well, *I* mean ' roped.' "

"And what *do* you mean, then, pray?"

"Well, confound it!—I beg your pardon—why, they made him ' safe,' of course."

"There now—you say he *was* safe; and yet why didn't he win?"

"Good gracious, Mrs. Softun, what an ignorant girl you must be! Don't you see they *squared* him—SQUARED him not to win; and so, how the deuce could he?"

* * * * *

I didn't go into the Church, after all; for Bessie didn't care much about it: and what with the Doctor's savings and Mamma's leavings, there was no great occasion for getting "japanned;" and so I left it alone. Turned my bucolics to account in rearing a good shaped Shorthorn or two for Smithfield, and varied their excellence with a few round-sterned Cochin Chinas, of the regular " prize-medal" breed. To be sure, when the good Doctor went over the place on his occasional visits to his dear daughter and esteemed son-in-law, he didn't "pass" all the stock with that word of approval he gave the sheep and cows in particular. There was, for instance, a clean-headed, ragged-quartered, old chesnut mare, of exceedingly aristocratic appearance, who walked about the paddocks with the air of everything else being under her, that completely bothered my worthy pastor and master as to what she was there at all for. I think it even took me some little trouble to explain to him how it was I had picked her up as likely to breed us a good sort of horse for "the phaeton."

The Gods forgive me for deceiving him! but if I had thought that mare could breed a buggy-horse, I would have cut her throat. She was by Emilius, foaled at Riddlesworth, and had run up for the Oaks of her year. And she didn't suit the collar, either; for the more the young one—by Kingston, he was—the more he grew, the less and less did they consider him fit for "the chaise." My wife was sure he was "too delicate;" and so I had to get rid of him at two years old, a bargain, to a neighbouring trainer, who took him—with a quiet understanding between ourselves that I was to pay so much per week for his "board and education."

And he turned out as full of promise as I could have hoped—and I had hoped a good deal for him, too, as I used to watch him just learning to strike out at home, when they thought I was estimating how many "stun," perhaps, one of the "Duke of Northumberland's" grand-daughters would reach on the block. The reports were all favourable. He was a good doer; then a good goer; and when I sneaked up to see him take his first spin, it was quite as much as "Snowy"—for so they called the white-headed lad who looked after him—could do from keeping him getting away with him. After that, we had "a taste," quite as satisfactory; and then my man, who was a terrible fellow for paying the "ex's," as he termed them, thought we might go in for a maiden plate. As the boy knew him, and I saw no great objection, they let "Snowy" have the mount; and then —like an ass, no doubt, as I was,—when I saw my wife's eye on the right column in the paper a day or two after, where it detailed that, at Such-and-such Spring Meeting, the City Members' Plate of, &c., &c., for horses that never, &c., &c., was won very cleverly by Mr. Smith's b. c. by Kingston, dam by Emilius, beating half-a-dozen others—then, I say, in the fulness of my heart, I confessed that *I* was Mr. Smith, and that the Kingston colt, the winner of the plate, was the little foal she had feared was too delicate to make a "four-wheeler."

The Messrs. Weatherby and Co. were not too hard on us; for, despite another plate and a chicken-hazard handicap to the credit side of the account, they let us in for one of the autumn events on very fair terms. At least we thought so, and accepted; and then other people began to think so too. The list-gentlemen named us in their bill of fare, with "prices marked against each article." Next, we came to be quoted at the Corner; and then, with just the matter-of-form understanding that, *if* he should, I promised something in the way of new-furnishing a drawing-room that made Bessie's eyes sparkle more, perhaps, than I had ever seen them since that eventful evening when I had asked her, with so much accompanying expression, "whether I might be *always* helping her over stiles?"

Ours wasn't what is called "a fashionable stable;" indeed, my trainer—a thin, wretched-looking man, whose own appearance rather went to confirm the idea—had got the credit for giving his horses more work than corn. I will, though, do him the justice to say that my colt thrived under the treatment, whatever it was, and came to the satisfactory * that announced his arrival at the scene of action, looking as bright and seeming as fit as a horse could be. My man, moreover, in that knowing, negative manner the thoroughly initiated express their opinions, confessed that he thought " the horse would not disgrace himself;" while one of the paper prophets boldly named him in the three the race was between; another, with less confidence, making him a " cock-boat."

If our "party" really had a failing, it was the unceasing war they, or rather he, waged against the " ex's " aforesaid. I should be afraid to say how many races he had lost by putting up his own lads, instead of experienced jockeys, or the wonderful sacrifices he submitted to in a variety of ways, to save a sovereign or two. Luckily, however, " Snowy " could hardly get the weight this time; and so we telegraphed a four-stone-nothing bit of humanity from Newmarket to take his place—a sober, serious child, with the head-piece of a man of fifty, and the bodily frame of a monkey. It was a great thing to get him; and the horse sprung a point or two in consequence. If it came to a finish now, we should have our fair chance for it—an assured fact that seemed amply satisfactory to everybody but " Snowy," who took his being passed over with anything but a good grace.

The last gallop over all right, and I left home on the morning of the race with visions of such curtains and such paperings dancing in Bessie's bright eyes, as she bade me good-bye and good luck, that none but Madame Vestris in the great days of the Lyceum could have thoroughly realized. I had some distance to go, and was rather late on the course—in time, though, to lay out a fifty for the stable, on the best terms I could. To accomplish this, I was introduced to a professional gentleman, who appeared to consider laying and taking the odds but the proper courtesies of civilized life. I never saw a man, in such a scene, so elaborately calm and studiously polite. In place of the restless, hyena-tramp of "the leviathan," the defiant clamour of my former friend the undertaker, or the "mock-auction" air and tone of too many others, he met you with the collected manner and stately attention of a Chesterfield. There was something all the more grateful in this, from his personal appearance scarcely leading you to expect it; for you must couple this gentle breeding with a squarish, rather coarsely-made man—a little down in one eye, I'm afraid, and looking altogether like a west-end publican or highly respectable butcher, who had taken to wearing his best clothes until he had at last got thoroughly used to them. He regretted extremely that he could not put me on at more than ten to one—about four points, as I afterwards found, under the price at the time; as sincerely hoped we might have a turn, "for my man really deserved it;" and so left me with a bow and a manner that made me feel under a deep obligation for all he had done for me.

I can't say much about the race myself, for I hardly understand it now; but something may be gathered from the comments on it as I caught them up. Little Struggles, for instance, as he waddled in to weigh, after it was over, wished to know, in extreme disgust, "why he had been brought all the way from home to ride such a rip as that?" *The Life*, again, devoted half-a-line to say that the Kingston colt, overpaced all the way, was "absolutely last;" while my courtly acquaintance, as he received the *rouleau,* observed, with an air of the sincerest sympathy, that he "was afraid the company was a little too good for me." Some few, however, were more explicit in their opinions; one pimply-faced gentleman, in particular, who owned to having been fool enough to put three sovereigns on, denouncing us bodily as "a set of thieves—" that "the horse was 'pulled,' as anybody could see—" that "he never ran a yard to win;" and that "it was a —(something)—robbery, and nothing else!"

* * * * *

To a certain extent, I must admit, he was right—as far as its being a—(something)—robbery, decidedly so. In the exhilaration consequent on three glasses of British brandy-and-water, "Snowy" was heard to declare that "*he'd* settled it. If he couldn't win on him, nobody else should; and they didn't either." A severe cross-examination on this avowal, with a police-court sketched in perspective, resulted in a deal of howling, and a partial confession. By the means of a worthy man who has since been difficult to trace, the disappointed "Snowy" got at his horse the night before the race, and so sacrificed our hopes of a good thing as effectually as he did his own character. As it was, we let him off too easily, with a "caution" in *The Calendar;* and he is now, I believe, on the strength of being "intimately connected with all the great stables," living comfortably enough on P. O. orders and postage-stamps, in some street, Lambeth.

Poor Bessie! it was a hardish blow for her at first, as women—bless them!—always think the best; and she made sure of winning, directly she knew she would win by it. I think it is nearly forgotten now, though some of the phrases acquired by that heartrending explanation turn up oddly enough at times. It was only the other day, at dinner, that she astonished the old Doctor tremendously by declaring it was her duty to tell me that she strongly suspected the new cook "stood in" with Evans the gardener—who don't live in the house—and that between them they "squared" the cold meat and table-beer to an alarming extent.

GOODWOOD,

IN THE DAYS OF THE LATE DUKE.

If one wished to impress the stranger with all the natural beauties, and at the same time the full splendour of an English home scene, we should surely take him to Goodwood! There is nothing else in the world like it. The varied features of the landscape—the glorious view that breaks upon the eye at every turn—the fresh breeze that greets you from the upland—the massive woods belting the horizon and offering a grateful shade to the approaching visitor—make up a combination of sylvan grandeur such as it would be vain to seek elsewhere. And we seek it *now*, not to indulge in the selfish luxury of solitude, but rather to share with others its many attractions and delights. It is high holiday once more on that princely domain, and hill and dale—the wide extending verdant sward—the quiet nook—the velvet slope—the pleasant path—and the winding road—are peopled with hurrying wayfarers and dotted with groups of smiling faces. Country neighbours are jogging on or stepping out. Middies from Spithead and "jollies" from Portsmouth jostle swells from Brighton, and "knowing" gentlemen from London. Here a lathy-looking lad takes advantage of an opening, and kicks his hack into a canter. There is a knack in that very "hustle" which tells tales of the racing stable; while at the next moment a busy cad has fastened on to the carriage-side, imploring you as the "noblest, and best, and luckiest of sportsmen," to have a card! It is the Cup Day, and another turn brings us well in front of the House, where peers and commoners, noble dames, and aspiring youths, are grouped again upon the lawn. That quiet-looking lord has his string of forty horses in work, and a good moiety of them here. This slim scion of nobility has a purple silk jacket already "smuggled" under his well-cut frock; and that honourable and gallant captain is as eagerly "engaged" as a belle at a ball, or a Queen's Counsel at an assize. Side-by-side with him saunters a Minister of State, and meeting them there limps up old "Dick Tattersall," with his pleasant voice and happy way with him; while a "foreigner of distinction" blazes away at a cigar as big as a walking-stick. These are the guests of the week, as indeed we all are. And no wonder our American cousins return home to talk tall of the days they spent at Goodwood; or that French Counts and German Princes betake themselves to their territories, resolved one day to win the prize here if money or brains, good management or good fortune, can find the horse to do it with. Even the "craving" leg

> "With nought but calculation in his brain,
> And nought revolving—but the way to gain,"

acknowledges to something of the enchantment of the scene, as he rises refreshed from his quiet lodging at Worthing or Bognor, ready and eager for the coming business of thirteen or fourteen "good betting" races before him; and, yet still so different does he feel are these in their conduct to the wild revelry of Epsom, the courtly elegance of Ascot, or the sober sameness of Newmarket Heath. We are come to enjoy our sport at the bidding of one of England's best of nobles, and so are bound to behave like gentlemen, or, at any rate, to try and pass, for the nonce, as honest men.

But that bidding we shall hear no more! That courteous unaffected welcome has at length died out from amongst us. The presiding spirit of the place, whose genial nature and kindly bearing went so far to complete the charm of the scene his hospitality had created, has been called away. It must be our duty to guard such a monument to his memory, and to show how a nobleman may attach himself to the precarious pursuits of the Turf, not only without shame or tarnish, but with ever-increasing honour to himself and to his House. If any instance were wanting to illustrate the condition of an English gentleman, we could scarcely bring a better than that of his Grace the Duke of Richmond, as he lived at Goodwood in the race week, sharing with others the sport he loved so well, and "diffusing its pleasures far and wide to thousands upon thousands of the less fortunate of his countrymen." The rise, in fact, of Goodwood as one of the great race meetings of the year is almost altogether identified with the career of the Duke. His Grace was born in 1791, and the first day's sport in the park took place in 1802. This was a Hunters' Stake, Farmers' Plate, gentleman-jockey kind of business, associated, no doubt, a good deal with the foxhounds then to be found in the famous home kennels. For seven or eight years more the meeting made but little advance, and in 1811 there were six races, with a match or two, and about a dozen of horses in all to make out two days of it. In the year following, however, the Duke, then Earl of March, attained his majority, and the Goodwood Cup was first instituted. Not that the heir could have had much to do with it in those days, for he was away to the wars with Wellington. On the conclusion of these, Lord March began at once to develop his taste for the Turf, and in 1817 came out at Goodwood with two horses in his own name, Princess and Hermes, winning his maiden race with the latter. By the next meeting he had a fair class "hunter-racer" called Roncesvalles, that carried him on for three or four seasons further. In 1819, he succeeded to the dukedom, consequent on the lamentable death of his father in Canada, from either the bite of a tame fox or a favourite dog, the actual cause having never been very satisfactorily shown. In two or three years more, the new Duke came gradually more and more to declare himself, and in 1823 boldly faced Newmarket with Pincushion; running second for the Oaks of the same year with Dandizette. The yellow jacket and scarlet cap were duly "coloured" in the Calendar, and by 1825 his Grace had quite a string of horses to his name. Goodwood was progressing proportionately, and the Goodwood Stakes established, the home stable running second for it. This was, indeed, rather a memorable year for the Park and its fortunes amongst the "places of sport." There was the Duke's brother, Lord William, riding well and riding winners, as we have since seen him do. And then there was a certain young Lord George Bentinck, making two dead heats of it in a cocked hat, and ultimately landing Olive a clever first for Mr. Poyntz. Goodwood began to look formidable enough by this: and in another season the racing was extended to three days, while the Duke was "coming" on his own account in very good form. With Frank Boyce for his favourite jockey, he landed the Stakes with that useful filly, Miss Craven, and took a taste of the great events at Epsom—both in

'27—with Gulnare for the Oaks, his neighbour Forth running second, and the "beautiful Brocard" third. They then got together such a team as Hindostan, Hindoo, The Alderman, Rough Robin, and Miss Craven, a company that found the Boyces and little Mr. Pavis plenty to do. Goodwood, in a word, had reached its glories. The Duke laid out thousands upon thousands in improving the course—the value of the several stakes was increased—and many new races originated. King George the Fourth sent his favourite mare Fleur-de-lis to win the Cup in 1829, which she did, beating the Derby horse Mameluke; and His Majesty won it again the year following with the same good mare, with Zinganee and The Colonel, also both the property of the King, the next to her. Then Priam took his two years' lease of it, and in 1833 the Goodwood week ran out to its four days full of sport. In the year but one after that we saw the Cup day in all its full splendour for the first time, when a white-legged Langar colt they called Elis came striding away for the Lavant; and James Robinson on the well-furnished Rockingham overcame the young Lord Chesterfield's Glaucus, the north-country St. Giles, and the blood-like Beiram for the Cup. What a scene they made of it! With the veteran Browne, the Lewes trainer, crying for joy, despite the rumour that the old Stockwell stockinger had gone to his last account before the race was run—with poor Beiram hobbling home through the crowd again—and pic-nic parties in the woods—and *rouge-et-noir* tables in full play—and high fashion on the Stand—and the good, brave, courteous duke, with a kind word for everybody, and a heart big enough to ask them all to come and stay with him, if he only had house-room to match it. But there were yet better times in store for Goodwood, when Mr.

Bowe and Grey Momus bloomed forth into "Lord George," and even Newmarket began to tremble at the issue. All the great things were going into Sussex, while all the Turf reforms and improvements were traceable to the same quarter. Defaulters were to be banished, mere gambling was to be abolished, time was to be kept, and good conduct to be enforced by all kinds of fines and penalties—and all on the system they had adopted at Goodwood. Even so, that when two noble lords of high degree, Lord Maidstone and Lord George himself, did get to the post to ride their match, they were fined five pounds each for being behindhand! The Duke of Richmond, however, did not confine himself and his horses by any means to their own district, but had just then four or five hard-wearing ones in work that he sent all over the country. There was the "everlasting" Confusionée, with pale, tiny, little Johnny Howlett on her, going day after day all the year round; together with Glenlivat, the King's Plate horses, Mus, and The Currier—and Tamburini, that Isaac Day afterwards turned to a good County Plate horse—with Sepoy and Guava, and so on. We have seen that yellow jacket and smart-tasselled cap travelling away with nearly all of them, at Egham, Oxford, and Abingdon—while Sam Rogers took the best of the business, and rode himself into repute upon them. There was Beggarman, too, that George Edwards had a fancy for, and transported to France, but only to bring him back to win the Goodwood Cup for his Royal master, the Duke of Orleans. Still, something like a return came of it when Mus won the Orleans Cup for the Duke the year following. And then Lord George broke with old John Day, and came over bodily ten thousand strong, and the glories of Goodwood get beyond all further record.

Charles XII. and Hyllus are running their "heads" and "heads;" Sweet Alice, with her level action, is stealing away from them; the Milesian O'Brien is flourishing in a perfect blaze of triumph; while calm, collected Lord George is winning or losing his thousands, all with the same imperturbable high-bred manner and expression. Somehow or other, the Duke rather declines as the other advances, but Kent can do some service for his good master yet: and Refraction wins the Oaks; and Red Deer runs away with the mite Kitchener and the Chester Cup; while Vampire lands the Ascot Stake two years in succession—all, be it understood, on their own account as the Duke's own, and in no sort of confederacy, as we believe, with Lord George and his leviathan establishment. The only partner the Duke of Richmond ever had on the Turf was his old friend Lord Stradbroke, and that was far earlier in his career. This was now gradually drawing to a close, with Flatman in the place of Rogers as the jockey of the stable, and Red Hart to win the Welcome, the Gratwicke, and the Duke Michael. The ticklish Red Hind, too, gave poor Nat a deal of trouble, and about the last great race his Grace won at home was the Chesterfield Cup in 1852 with Harbinger. The next season saw him out, and Pharos was one of the last horses that ever carried his colours to the post. Following the example of Lord George, the Duke made an offer of his stud in a lot to Messrs. Payne and Greville, but it was not closed with; and towards the end of 1853 he sold five of his brood mares—Refraction, Cuckoo, Officious, Reel, and another to M. Lupin, for France. The horses in training were brought to the hammer in the succeeding spring, since when the Duke never had a racehorse. Lords Henry and Alexander Lennox occasionally kept a nag or two with Kent afterwards, but even these are gone, and the stables as empty as the kennels long have been. The elder Kent still lives at the latter, but he has two or three farms in hand, and has taken prizes for his Southdowns.

The Duke himself was equally famous as an agriculturist as a sportsman. He was far away the most popular man in England with the farmers, and deservedly so, too. The same unaffected manner distinguished him amongst them; and it was quite a treat to see him preside at the annual Smithfield Club dinner, of which he was the life President. His great opponent here was his neighbour, Mr. Rigden, of Hove, and continual were the challenges they were throwing out to each other, as the award had been for or against them. But the Duke's Downs are by far the most *thorough-bred* looking of their kind. They have beauty with substance, but without that evident alloy with which the Southdown has been *improved* into something bigger and coarser. "Old Charley," the shepherd, is still full of pride for his flock, as the present duchess has always taken a great interest in them. Her noble husband has long put aside the cap and jacket in which, as Lord March, he at one time was wont to perform so well; but the world looked anxiously to him for the Goodwood week, a hope which has not been disappointed.

The late Duke began life as an active sportsman, in the more direct interpretation of the time. He was a cricketer, an excellent shot, and a good man over a country. His wound, however, interfered with these pursuits, and he never kept hounds himself. It is now nearly fifty years since the cheery note of one has disturbed the echoes of the Goodwood kennel. There was then a very clever pack of hounds at Goodwood, but their fate, according to old Tom Grant, their huntsman, was, indeed, a sad one. In 1813 the then Duke " gave them to the King to hunt calves, or donkeys, or something of that sort; what a pity they should have come to what they did !"

On every showing there is a good man lost to us. As an honour to his Order, as a landlord, a neighbour, a good soldier, and a good citizen, the Duke of Richmond was alike to be lamented. We have seen him, as we have endeavoured to picture him, the munificent host of that great Goodwood Carnival. We have heard his character spoken to as we have driven through his estates in North Britain. We have watched him in more recent times wake up at the old war cry, and march through the streets of Edinburgh at the head of his regiment to meet his sovereign. We have joined in when men rose again and again to welcome him as the farmers' friend. And of all we have seen and all we have heard there was but one echo—the Duke of Richmond was worthy of his rank and of his fortunes, and a "noble man" in the first and best reading of the word.

THE BANISHED MAID.

A LAMENT ON THE GAME OF SKITTLES BEING PUT A STOP TO BY
THE AUTHORITIES IN LEICESTERSHIRE.

The steady rain comes drizzling down,
The swells are haunting Leicester town,
Alas! that Dian now should frown
   Upon a Banished Maid!

Her nags in fettle fit to go,
Her will as good the way to show,
Ye Gods! avert the coming blow
   Upon a Banished Maid.

Or Nimrod! from thy history dim
That fatal day, when, Queen of Whim,
They sentenced thee in judgment grim
   To be a Banished Maid.

Forlorn she goes—they find—they fly!
When hark! how grows that thrilling cry—
Once more she'll either do or die,
   Although a Banished Maid.

Shall those broad pastures plead in vain?
One yawner set her right again;
Once more she's mistress of the plain,
   And not a Banished Maid.

A moment take, while yet you may,
The wonted pleasures of the day,
For cruel fate still bids you *nay!*
   And be a Banished Maid.

No more the pounded ask a lead—
No more the faithful race for speed—
There's many a gallant heart will bleed
   All for the Banished Maid.

Godiva's self, without her stays,
Not half the charms to mortal gaze,
When mounted for her ride displays,
   As does the Banished Maid.

Time was when Theobald o'er " the Vale "
In all her pride of place would sail;
No ruthless edict made her quail,
   Or be a Banished Maid.

Or, when the staggers met at Slough,
And Davis gave his welcome bow;
With Gilbert pleasure at the prow
   Was not a Banished Maid.

That stately chesnut oft would show
How she could pace it down the row,
While fair-haired Freke could sit her so,
        Unlike a Banished Maid.

Still, virtue triumphant will prevail,
Though Gentle Will would join our bail,
And ask, are there no cakes and ale
        E'en for a Banished Maid?

Irate, old Christmas strikes the ground,
Quick! in an iron grasp 'tis bound,
And lost is life with Horse and Hound,
        When lost the Banished Maid.

[The long and severe frost of January, 1861, followed immediately on the enforcement of this edict.]

A DECEIVING HORSE.

"And what are you doing with the Oliver horse, sir?"

"Well, anything and everything; hack him, and hunt him, and so on."

"And can he jump at all?"

"Yes, that he can! He is a good flying-fencer; and nothing I ever put him at yet has either turned him or troubled him."

"Come, sir, now I'll tell you what I'll do. He had hardly pace enough over the flat, though he would last for ever. You send him up to my place, sir, for a month or two, and we'll see if he can't pull off a steeplechase handicap, or a hurdle-race. If he does, we'll divide it; and if he don't, I'll stand you harmless for the wear and tear of his teeth."

"So be it. When will you have him?"

"The sooner the better. I suppose there's not a deal to get off him, for he never carried much flesh!"

"N-o-o—he's just in good hard-working condition."

The speaker who made this handsome proposal was our old friend Dominie, the trainer; while the other "party" to the dialogue was a country gentleman, who dearly loved a bit of racing, if there wasn't too much to pay for it. The Oliver horse had been rather a sore subject in this way; as he had run second, third, and fourth for a year and a-half all over the country, until his very travelling bill was something considerable, but without even the set-off of a solitary "fifty" to be placed against it. However, another such a chance at no cost was not to be resisted; and the worthy owner, Mr. Wilson, left the Stand in which this conversation took place, determined to start the bay off again for Thistley Downs the very next morning, as he was only "eating his head off" at home.

The Oliver horse certainly did not look in a likely way to accomplish this extraordinary feat; and his "hard-working condition" had a good deal of literal truth about it, for he was little better than a bag of bones, as he had been by no means pampered on his return from that unprofitable tour in the provinces. Still he would, of course, be all the readier to go on with; and the odd man of the establishment was soon hunted up.

"Here, Jack, I want you to take the bay horse up to Mr. Dominie's again. You had better start the first thing to-morrow morning. How long will it take you?"

"Be I to walk with un?"

"O, yes; go right across the country, you know."

"Well, a couple of days—leastways we shall have to be out one night on it."

"The deuce you will! Then I'll tell you what you must do. Get on with him to-morrow as far as Pentybwywn, and ask my friend, Mr. Carre, to give the horse a berth for the night, while you can put up in the town. You know Mr. Carre; he keeps the hounds there, and we have got a puppy of his here now. One good turn deserves another."

"Yes, sir; and be I to take any clothes for the horse, or anything of that sort?"

"No, no; Mr. Dominie will find all that. Only put on an old stable-bridle to lead him with."

"Very well, sir," said Jack, who would have preferred a rug to *ride* him with; but started next day as directed, and arrived in due course at Pentybwywn. Mr. Carre's place was a good two miles out; and at the close of a dull dark November day Jack led old Oliver up to the stables.

"Mr. Carre at home?"

"Well, he has not got home again yet. What may you want with him?"

"I was to leave this here horse from Mr. Wilson's— Mr. Wilson of the Fogge House."

"Oh, ah! I know; him as has got one of our Dorimonts. Well, you can leave him with me, and I shall take precious good care of him you may be certain. Would you like a horn of ale before you start again?"

Naturally Jack would like a horn of ale, or two, or three, if it came to that, before he went in search of his own quarters; soon after when the squire came in from shooting.

"Anything fresh, Evans, since morning?"

"Nothing partickler, sir; Mr. Wilson, as has got Harmony at walk, has sent a horse in."

"That's all right—very much obliged to him, I'm sure; just, too, when you'll know where to put him."

And the Squire went in to dinner; and Evans, who was huntsman, and foreman, and all that sort of thing, proceeded to make his arrangements for the morrow before it got quite dark.

* * * * *

The Squire was an early man, and in the kennels by times the next morning, when Jack again turned up.

"Morning, sir."

" Good morning to you; and what may it be you want?"

For Jack's " personal " was not very prepossessing; and Mr. Carre had too many hangers-on from the town to give much encouragement to any of the sort.

" If you please, sir, I come from Mr. Wilson with that horse last night, and "—

" Yes, yes, I heard of it. And how is Mr. Wilson, and how is Harmony, eh?"

" Measter is tidy, thank you, sir, and the little bitch as fat as butter."

" That's all right. Well, give my compliments and best thanks to your master, and "—as Jack still hesitated—" here is something for yourself."

" THANKEE, sir," said Jack, with a very marked emphasis on his words; for he had really got more than he expected, however open he was to handling a half-crown or two. Still he readily put it down to his care of the puppy; and went on to ask of Evans where he should find his horse?

" Your WHAT?" said the Squire, utterly eclipsing Jack's own emphasis of expression.

"The horse, sir—the horse I brought here last night."

" Yes, yes, we all know that; and what then?"

" Why then, sir, I be to take 'un on this morning to Mr. Dominie's, at Thistley."

" What in the world were you going to take him there for? Dominie has no want for flesh."

" No, sir, not as I knows on; but they be going to put 'un to work again."

Evans looked hard at the Squire, and the Squire looked as hard at Jack.

" By Jove! my man, I'm afraid we've put 'un to work again in a way you hardly bargained for. Here, do you think you should really know your horse now if you saw him?"

"In course I should, sir," said Jack.

And the Squire led the road to the boiling-house. He took up a leg of beef as he got there. The Oliver horse had a white heel, and Jack turned deadly pale. The Squire said nothing, but beckoned him out into the paddock, where, under the elms, amongst other relics, was the head of a horse evidently fresh slaughtered. The Squire commented on this in a slow ominous tone of voice.

"Once more, I say, young man, give my best thanks and compliments to your master. I am afraid there has been rather a serious mistake here ; but we were very short of flesh, and you were not over explicit as to what you wanted of us. However, it will be a satisfaction to your master to know that he will never drop another tenner over this poor beggar; and so, anyhow, we have saved him some money, and you some trouble."

· * ⁂ * * ⁂

Jack got through his message as best he might; but he was in want of a situation on Saturday ; and Harmony, with five-and-sixpence to pay, was delivered by the carrier in the course of the week, with a parchment label round her neck, embodying Mr. Wilson's "best compliments and thanks."

THE GREAT HORSE AND HOUND SHOW, IN YORKSHIRE.

AGRICULTURAL Societies are getting more and more ambitious of their attractions. They are no longer content with the simple essentials of a cattle show proper—the placid Shorthorn, the beefy Hereford, the trim Southdown, or that martyr monster of hog's flesh, whose continued existence seems to centre on the undisturbed half-hour's repose so necessary after rather too hearty a dinner. With due consideration for our wives and daughters, poultry and flowers have come to a recognised place in the programme; although one high-born dame will feed her own pork, and another unglove her jewelled hand to try the touch of a Duchess heifer. Then, have we seen at the Sparkenhoe Club a row of shepherds' dogs ranged side by side with the fleecy Leicesters and towering Cotswolds; while a handsome colley put forth his intelligent head, conscious, as it were, of his many personal advantages over his merely useful bob-tailed opponents. At Birmingham a counter display of pointers, setters, and Clumbers has carried us bodily out of Bingley Hall into the Repository; and at Boston, a few years back, a baby show in the morning, and a round of fireworks in the evening, helped out the anniversary of the North Lincolnshire Association. Never shall we forget the utter despondency, the weary, hope-broken attitude of one unsuccessful exhibitor, as she sat in a corner of that dog-hole of a coffee-room with an uncommended "kid" in her lap. Her John himself had long since deserted her, and was off to hear Pishey Snaith sing the praises of old Theon, or to see what "the Captain" would pick out in the way of a hunter.

And here, after all, should be the companion attractions of beeves and flocks. Here, in fact, is one of the strongest points of such a gathering. Only mark how the rush of visitors crowd round the "nags," and hearken how their first question is as to which thorough-bred horse has got the prize? And yet, strange to say, no section of the show has progressed so slowly. The Royal Agricultural Society, indeed, appeared to think it almost a sin to encourage such an exhibition, and got out of it again and again by all sorts of side winds. Let the Mayor here, or the locals there, offer a premium for that Englishman's boast, a well-bred horse, but the Council would have nothing to do with it. They have at length, to be sure, been fairly bullied into re-establishing the class under the direct auspices of the Society; but, as may be supposed, with such apathetic assistance no great deal has come of it. There has never yet been a thoroughly good entry of hunter stallions, although now and then a horse like Hobbie Noble or a British Yeoman would offer them the example. The finest field we ever saw was in Ireland, at Waterford, mainly through the offices of that good sportsman, Captain Croker, who afterwards instituted the Challenge Cup; but some undue interference upset the award, and the worst horses succeeded to the best places. The West of England does little in this way, and the East for years was content with an annual peep at the same handsome little chesnut—Captain Barlow's Revenge, a horse that had the credit of carrying Sir Tatton on many a long journey, and upon which he was painted. In a word, if you wish to see "a horse show," you must go into Yorkshire. They have not only a better sample, but they know far better how to display it. With their well-arranged rings, the judges in the centre, and the public on the outside of the rails, there can be no greater treat to a sportsman than to see a dozen or so of thoroughbred ones thus put upon parade. And we have enjoyed it over and over again; perhaps more at Malton than elsewhere, when the active, lusty Burgundy beat Galaor, St. Lawrence, Fugleman, Pigskin, and others. Still, as a rule, the very first-class have been kept back, although there is scarcely a district which the Yorkshire Society has visited but that had a really good one or two handy. Either the honour or the stake was not worth having, and so such fairish second-raters as Canute, Spencer, and Dr. Sangrado were fighting their battles over and over again.

At this juncture, with a spirit eminently characteristic of its conduct, the little Cleveland Society came to the rescue. It boldly broke the egg by associating an entry of foxhounds with its pristine endeavours in the way of encouraging the breeds of cattle and sheep. So signal a success did this at once become, so readily was the echo taken up, that Cleveland determined to do a little more, and see if it could not be famous for a horse as well as a hound show. The experiment came to an issue, with a result in every way proportionate to the energy and liberality with which it was set about. The committee began by offering a premium of one hundred sovereigns—far more than ever was given before—for the best thoroughbred stud horse, having served mares during the season 1860, which, in the opinion of the judges, "is best calculated to improve and perpetuate the breed of the sound and stout thorough-bred horse, not only for racing, but also for general stud purposes." There was another prize of twenty sovs. for the second-best; and good accommodation promised in the yard, with a roomy box, made perfectly comfortable and secure for each horse. This promise was fully carried out. The boxes alone, either for room or warmth, were worth going all the way to see, and a horse might have lived as well in them for two or three months as for two or three nights. Then the committee announced further that " three gentlemen of the highest reputation, soundest judgment, and strictest impartiality, should be selected to make the awards—one being a nobleman or gentleman connected with the Turf, another an experienced trainer of race-horses, and the third a gentleman who has a thorough knowledge of breeding horses for both racing and hunting purposes." Every exhibitor had the privilege of suggesting the names of gentlemen to act as judges; but the committee of course reserved the right of selection. On a Thursday morning, then, early in August 1860, the now flourishing town of Middlesbro'-on-Tees, although not so long since but a few farmhouses, was the scene of some considerable excitement. The entry, to number not fewer than twenty nominations, was known to have filled, while no end of high-mettled horses were rumoured to be in. At a little before twelve the yard, or rather the somewhat swampy show ground, was opened, and soon after, having taken a walk through the boxes, their worships " stepped into the ring." The gentleman connected with the Turf turned up in Mr. James Weatherby; Tom Dawson, of Middleham, was the experienced trainer; and Mr. Hobson, of Kettleby Thorpe, near Brigg, the breeder of that chance horse, North Lincoln, accompanied them as a gentleman with a thorough knowledge of breeding horses both for racing and hunting purposes. The ring is not large enough to have the eighteen here of the twenty-one entered out at once, even if all their tempers would have stood this, and a very imposing sight is consequently lost to the anxious audience, who, catalogue in hand, are watching the award. The judges themselves, by the exercise of a little moral fiction, are not assumed to know the names of any of the horses that come before them, but are instructed to talk in cypher of what they think of No. 1 when compared with No. 2, and so on. Soon do they ask for that *Number One* accordingly, and out there bursts with a flourish, scattering the patient Dobbins waiting for their prize-shoes, about the very biggest thorough-bred horse in all England. His substance is certainly extraordinary, and he has been a prize horse before to-day. It is Hunting Horn, a high-priced yearling at Doncaster, and the first prize horse for getting hunters at the Warwick meeting of the Royal Agricultural Society. But he has only grown coarser since then, his action is not taking, and there is altogether a little too much of him. The Tykes will not have him; but the foreigners, it is thought, may, and they are already nibbling at the thousand or two that Wadlow is asking. *Number Two*, Ethelbert, said to have grown into a magnificent horse, does not put in an appearance; and we have, as second out, the pretty Motley, with his blooming coat, his good top, and a head the very image of old Touchstone. But there is rather too *little* of him; and the judges pass on to the common-looking, heavy-shouldered, fumbly-going Tirailleur, a horse that his owner very gamely sent all the way from Kent, where we just previously saw him on inspection, although, of course, without distinction. However, the Austrians have got him at a long figure, and one gives a sigh of relief to think he is gone. "The next lot," as they say at "the Corner," is of very different *calibre*, and long is he under examination. The conditions are for the best stallion to get horses, not only for racing but more general purposes. A difficult combination of excellence may-be, but surely this is something like it. Mr. Weatherby strokes his chin as if he was hard hit at last; Dawson scans the nag leerily round, and Mr. Hobson bids the man "walk him down." He does that well enough, and there is a murmur of approval round the ring at his action. It is a child of old Alice, as they fondly call her—the Lord Fauconberg, with his bloodlike head, fine forehand, and famous back and quarters. He does not look quite so full of flesh as when we saw him in Scotland, but there is quality and substance there if you like, and, but for that Birdcatcher hock, what shall beat him? However, he took the first prize at the Great Yorkshire meeting at Pontefract, and as his Lordship leaves the ring it is clear enough he has made an impression, with takers of three to one that he is first or second; and they cannot be far out either, for he must be at all points one of the most "fashionable" of the lot. But he is hardly out ere he is forgotten, for, with a "*hie! hie!* there!" in marches the great horse of the country. And at the first glance we know that our chief fear is groundless. Voltigeur has only fined as he has aged, and he is not nearly so coarse an animal now as when he won the Derby. Every trace of "the Yorkshire coach-horse" is gone, and he stands there in high condition, the very embodiment of the powerful, muscular, and sound blood stallion.

"Look at them legs and hocks, as clean as when hur was foaled!"

"And think what he done, too!"

"He beat Dootchman, and won t'Leger."

"Aye mon, and he got Védette, the best on 'em out for many a long day."

"Nay, but *hur's a bonny horse,*" adds a fourth, as a climax, grinding away at the stem of his pipe in that ecstasy of delight which, perhaps, a Yorkshireman only can can feel to the full, when he has all his eyes on a good one.

And he is a bonny horse, too; so fresh and so good almost everywhere, that one hardly dares to hint that his head is not quite handsome, or that he may get a trifle light in the girth. The now only remaining signs of any coarseness are just "fore and aft." He is what a houndsman would call rather "throaty" in the setting on of the head, and he has a thick dock that does not come well away from his quarters. These are otherwise capital; and anyhow he will leave his legs as an offering to his country; whilst, as he lashes out playfully in his light, straight trot, people feel already that it is over—even on Voltigeur against the field! Still, his stable companion is a neat one, the long, low, and level Fandango, the evenest horse of the lot, and that looks bound to walk away with a loose rein directly you drop your hand to him. He might show a little more blood, but, as it is, Lord Zetland for first and second is by no means so impossible; and *Number Seven* has many a benè mark against him. The light, elegant, hollow-backed Backbiter is soon passed; the Wild Huntsman does not show; and The Hadji, a very good-looking horse already, has only to thicken and furnish into something more, and Mr. Groves may fix many a white favour on his bridle.* The stilty Claret is duly presented at this great levée on his return from Ireland; and then Windhound, the acknowledged sire of Thormanby, the Derby winner, immense in his power and blood-like in his appearance, is called. But somehow or other he does not please either judges or jury; those quarters and hind-legs are not liked, and he leaves with the foregone conclusion that we shall see no more of him. Over De Clare there is a far more serious conference, and his merits and drawbacks make out the longest "case" of the whole assize. He has grown into a wonderfully grand horse, and seems bound to get weight-carriers, but he has the fatal defect of badly-placed shoulders, and these no doubt stopped him. Still De Clare has backers, and their Lordships are strangely loth to let him go again. But what a contrast, as they meet, is he to the corky, varmint, cheerful, hard-wearing Farnham, with his frightfully fired fore-legs, the one "shutter-up," and not an ounce of flesh on his body. And note how quickly that one eye of his finds the furze fence the hunters are to jump, and how ready he is to face it. He has topped many a one in his time, but that is scarcely the thing now; and so by him and Dr. Sangrado, the pleasant old-fashioned style of hunter that Marshall might have painted, we hasten on to something of a little higher form. It is here ready served in a moment, like the next "remove" at a well-put dinner, when the appetite seems to pall a little at the more substantial dishes. How nicely timed it does come to be sure, and how one does enjoy the change, after so much of the big, beefy Windhounds and De Clares, to that neat, handsome, sweet bit of a racehorse,

---

* The Hadji won the first prize at the All-Yorkshire Show a season or two after this was written.

Saunterer—"the black 'un," as the legs called him, the truest made horse of them all, with his well-knit back, his fine shoulders, his wicked little head, and thin, blood-like neck. And then those legs, not big ones, your lordships, for he is not a big one anywhere, but as clean as paint, and as hard as iron. Turn back to your *Calendars*, erudite Mr. Weatherby, and trace all he has done. Go back to memory, Mr. Dawson, or ask your next-door neighbour all he could do; and you, Squire Jaques—the "melancholy Jaques" for once, as you stand by him in the box and reflect how readily you "got out" of him. "He aint big enough for *'em!*" comment the knowing North Ridingers, with a palpable emphasis on the abbreviated *'em*; while we fear terribly this contemptuous tone is directed especially to the judges. The plain coaching Neville can never do after that; and Cavendish, a better nag to show as one would fancy, is kept at home. The Cure, however, an old friend hereabouts, has a heartier welcome, while the trio hang to him nearly as long as they did to De Clare. He is certainly a fine-topped "big little horse," wearing wonderfully well for his age and all he has done, and full more of muscle than flesh. Mr. Hobson is especially struck with him, and gazes on him more as a new love than an old friend. If he had only a prop under him "to perpetuate the breed of the sound and stout!"—but, alas! his forelegs absolutely bend and tremble as he tries to stand still! And as one looks at them, so bad are they now that it is hard to imagine they could ever have been good. Yet The Cure has his party, as he makes way for the lathy Hospitality and the big-barrelled, short-tailed General Williams, a good racehorse fashioned into a hunter, but not quite up to the Middlesbro' mark of any such association of excellence.

Half an hour is now supposed to elapse for the judges to savage their well-earned sandwich, and then half a dozen of the elect are summoned for a second trial. These are—5. Lord Fauconberg, 6. Voltigeur, 7. Fandango, 13. De Clare, 16. Saunterer, and 19. The Cure. De Clare and Saunterer are then drafted back to their boxes, and Voltigeur put on one side by himself. The public see in a moment what this means, and Mr. Booth begins to collect all the even half-crowns he has been laying. Lord Fauconberg, Fandango, and The Cure thus stand in for second, and common opinion seems to rank them as they are here named. But a heavy storm, always due sooner or later at Middlesbro', breaks over the town, when the horses are ordered in, and the note of a hound from an adjoining tent seems all at once to remind people how much they have been neglecting that part of the entertainment. When it clears a little the horse judges are found to have left the ground, solemnly sworn not to divulge their award until after the committee dinner—the only mistake in this otherwise well-managed meeting. Hundreds who have paid the highest price on the best day are thus sent home again without being able to say what has won. The crowning excitement of the thing is utterly spoilt, and all to tempt one to what turned out to be a terribly slow, badly-served dinner. It was not until after another walk through the boxes on the next morning that we were enabled to fashion our list into a really ship-shape return, and here it is:—

A Plate of 100 sovs., with 20 for the second, given by the Cleveland Agricultural Society for the best thoroughbred stud horse, having served mares during the season 1860, best calculated to improve and perpetuate the breed of the sound and stout thorough-bred horse, not only for racing, but also for general purposes; entrance 5 sovs. each, 2 of which were returned to every one but the winner; 21 entries.

THE HORSE AND THE HOUND SHOW. 143

Lord Zetland's br. Voltigeur, by Voltaire out of Martha Lynn, by Mulatto, 13 yrs. 1

Mr. J. Ashton's b. The Cure, by Physician out of Morsel, by Mulatto 19 yrs. 2

Mr. M'Adam's b. Lord Fauconberg, by Irish Birdcatcher out of Alice Hawthorne, by Muley Moloch, 10 yrs.—Highly Commended.

Lord Zetland's b. Fandango, by Barnton out of Castanette, by Don John, 8 yrs.—Highly Commended.

Mr. J. Merry's bk. Saunterer, by Irish Birdcatcher out of Ennui, by Bay Middleton, 6 yrs.

Mr. J. Peart's b. De Clare, by Touchstone out of Miss Bowe, by Catton, 8 yrs.

(The two next, though not placed.)

Mr. J. Wadlow's br. Hunting Horn, by Surplice out of Ferina, by Venison, 6 yrs. 0

Mr. T. M. Hutchinson's b. Motley, by Touchstone, dam by Lanercost, 9 yrs... 0

Mr. J. Kitchen's br. Tirailleur, by Voltigeur out of Tally, by Melbourne, 5 yrs 0

Mr. T. Sutcliffe's br. Backbiter, by Gladiator or Don John out of Scandal, by Selim, 15 yrs. 0

Mr. T. Groves' b. The Hadji, by Faugh-a-Ballagh out of Athol Brose, by Orlando, 5 yrs. 0

Mr. T. Groves' br. Claret, by Touchstone out of Mountain Sylph, by Belshazzar, 8 yrs. 0

Mr. T. Groves' br. Windhound, by Pantaloon out of Phryne, by Touchstone, 13 yrs. 0

Mrs. J. Scott Waring's ch. Farnham, by Ratcatcher out of Lunette, by Figaro, 16 yrs. 0

Mr. S. Kirby's b. Dr. Sangrado, by Physician out of Sweetbriar, by Langar, 19 yrs. 0

Mr. W. Robinson's b. Neville, by Napier out of Sally Snobs, by Sandbeck, 9 yrs. 0

Mr. J. Ridley's br. Hospitality, by Malcolm out of Envy, by Perion, 7 yrs. 0

Mr. W. Hudson's b. General Williams, by Womersley out of Lady Elizabeth, by Sleight of Hand, 6 yrs 0

Mr. W. Gulliver's ch. Ethelbert, by Faugh-a-Ballagh out of Espoir, by Liverpool, 10 yrs.; Mr. J. M'Adam's b. Wild Huntsman, by Harkaway out of Honey Dear, by Plenipotentiary, 9 yrs.; and Mr. W. Robinson's br. Cavendish, by Voltigeur out of The Countess of Burlington, by Touchstone, 4 yrs., were entered, but not sent.

It will be seen that two of the best tried stud horses, Voltigeur, the sire of Védette and Skirmisher, and The Cure, the sire of Lambton and Underhand, were placed first and second, the only other horse that could cope with them in this way being Windbound. The younger horses—such as Saunterer, Fandango, or even Lord Fauconberg—may be rated as almost altogether untried. The judges, however, had to decide by what they see before them, and to "perpetuate the sound and the stout;" they certainly selected as second best the most infirm horse of the whole entry. There is no disguising the fact that this award did not give satisfaction, while every one went with Voltigeur as the winner. This is the first time, we believe, Lord Zetland's horse was ever on a show ground; but we met The Cure some years since at the Royal Society's meeting at Carlisle, when he and The British Yeoman were both put aside for the lady's-palfry-looking Ravenhill, one of the grossest mistakes ever committed, although by no means the only one. Either Lord Fauconberg or Fandango would have been much more acceptable, but the judges were said to be unanimous in the opinion they arrived at as to The Cure looking like getting sound and stout stock.

Another challenge from "Noisy," with a scarlet coat or two grouped about the door way, leads us to where the four ex-M.F.H. have had a comparatively quiet morning on the well-laid flags. These "learned brothers" sitting in the "other court" were Mr. Hodgson,* the "Tommy Hodgson" of the Holderness, but who tried his hand for a season or two in Leicestershire; Mr. Lee Steere, from the Horsham; Mr. Williamson, of the Durham; and Mr. Mark Milbank, of the Bedale. There were premiums for puppies, for three season hunters, and for single stallion hounds; while the kennels represented included the Cleveland, the Durham County, the Sinnington, Lord Middleton's, the Hon. G. W. Fitzwilliam's, and Mr. Hill's. The Cleveland show of foxhounds was not a great one, but there were some very good hounds amongst them, and one or two especially handsome. We thought we never saw a nicer draft than Lord Middleton's as they left the horse ring on the second day, and if they run pretty well up to this stamp they must be a fine kennel of hounds to look over. The dog and bitch puppies showed immense power and substance, standing on a short leg, and very handsomely marked. The dog hound Harper, substituted for Royster, is by Hardwicke, who won the prize at Redcar. The bitch, again, in the older class was super-excellent, but her companion in the couples has not equal power, or Morgan might have stood even higher than he did here. The judges were, indeed, much inclined to think that hounds would show better in the absence of any proviso for one of each sex being entered together. Amongst the stallions Lord Middleton was also in favour, but more with the public generally than the judges, who gave it against him. But his Lordship's was a wonderfully showy hound, as handsome as a picture, and until you went into it closely, altogether a finer dog than the Durham Splendour, with which Harrison

---

* Mr. Hodgson died since this was written.

pocketed his flask. Splendour, however, will stand looking into, his colour, a light grey and white, being the chief thing against him : for although a half-faced hound, the shape and the head itself are altogether perfect. Then, he has famous deep shoulders, with a deal of liberty, while he girths half an inch more than Morgan's, to the surprise of many who thought the latter clearly the bigger round. Splendour stands rather over three-and-twenty inches in height, while he runs out thirty and a-half in "circumference." But it wants a houndsman to quite appreciate him, and an injury he has received in the stern tends to spoil the 'effect of any " first impression." An old-fashioned white hound from the Cleveland, called Primate, and a famous one in his own country, still did not tell here, and the other two had it all to themselves. But the Cleveland had some fine hounds in their entry; and Mr. Hill's Dashwood was as good-looking as anything, big in the bone, and of a rare wearing black and tan colour, with a capital dog's head, but the bitch was not quite worthy of him. However, they took the tankard, and Ben Morgan, for Lord Middleton, the horn —a hardish one to blow as it seemed, and although Sebright and two or three more did get a note out of it, Mr. Parrington beat them all for a good long telling *blast* that proclaimed he was away ! But the Secretary is to hunt the Hurworth next season, so that he is only getting himself into proper pipe ; while last year he took the prize whip as the best man over the timber they put up at Redcar. Surely no man was ever so qualified for the official duties of a Horse and a Hound Show. Tom Sebright got his spurs for the second best puppies with a couple of nicely-shaped, handsomely marked young hounds, although not so fine in the shoulder or good in the neck as "My Lord's" which were all over of a nicer stamp, though we fancy Tom himself thought otherwise. But as varmint Jack Parker says, "If we were all Lords we should all have prizes of some sort!" and the Sinnington show as much sport as any of them, though they are rather tall, rambling-looking hounds to the eye, with hardly bone enough for their height. But Jack met his fortunes with great philosophy, whether it were with Clinker and Ariel, at Middlesbro', or riding over the furze fences at Helmsley—a kind of amusement he thinks they will go on with in Yorkshire "till they have to call in the C'rowner."

This was enacted in great form at Middlesbro' on the second day, with a grand stand at half-a-crown a head to see the fun from; and a lunch discreetly set an hour or so previous, to steady the nerves of the competitors and their anxious friends and relatives. The fences were very sporting-looking ones—a well built hedge, and then a five-foot rail to get out with; while the reality of the thing was immensely increased by a wonderfully well got up old Yorkshire farmer, who, every time a horse made a mistake, walked up, spud in hand, to see what damage they had done him. The jumping was almost generally good, and two or three awkward horses very well handled. Mr. Parrington, the secretary, took both the prizes for the best hunting gelding and mare; and King Charming, a very clever one, only wanting in a little more "style," was also the winner at Redcar; while his chief opponent now was a very good-looking chesnut by Dagobert, whose rider and owner, young Mr. Batty, had the word of everybody as the best horseman. In repose, his seat was by no means perfect, but when he set the chesnut going, they were quite at home together, and the way in which he took the young one over the rails quite a treat to see. But this jumping business, in cold blood, is not altogether a sight for a sportsman, especially on a damp drizzling day, with men and horses that are or have been about wet through, and that come to their work chilled and starved. Some of them wanted a deal of warming, and Mr. Jackson's horse, for one, went round, all for the lack of a little more rousing.

The Cleveland mares were very excellent, though they are often crossing these, even for carriage horses, into "something better;" and the two and three-year-old hunting stock were almost generally remarkable for their good action. In a word, the horse show, try it where you would, was of that extent and character which no district but one somewhere in Yorkshire could furnish. And the Middlesbro' was essentially a horse show. It was said there were pigs and sheep and cattle on the ground, which we trust their friends were able to find. But nine-tenths of the public came to see the horses and hounds, and looked at, and talked of, and thought of nothing else, save, perhaps, the horse-shoeing, at which some twenty sons of Vulcan went to work; but they were capped on a vast deal too fast, and, when only too late, discovered that those who had done first had not done best. In the whole art and mystery of farriery more horses have been injured from being shod in a hurry than from any other cause. The men clearly did not know what was wanted, and for the future they must point out the line a little clearer.

That a creditable or a really excellent show of thorough-bred stallions can be got together is thus an established fact. Let us make it a precedent. With liberal premiums, good management, and efficient judges, there may be many more such. We would, indeed, go so far as to directly suggest to the Master of the Horse that one of the most popular steps the Government could take would be the annual offer of a Royal Plate of 100 guineas for the best thorough-bred stallion calculated to get sound and stout stock. Such countenance would tend to do a vast deal of good, and gradually to put the right stamp of merit on the right sort of horses. It would not be the winner only which would be served by such an exhibition, while the great question would be, into whose hands the conduct of the business should be entrusted? If the Jockey Club be not precisely the authority, the Royal Agricultural Society has, we fear, so far shown itself scarcely worthy of the trust. Still, such a hint from high places might stir up the Council to better things.

> "I scorn a patron, though I condescend
> Sometimes to call a Minister my friend."

[This was in 1860, and at the meeting of the Royal Agricultural Society, in the following summer at Leeds, the example here cited was adopted, and £100 premium given for the best thorough-bred horse. It was won by Mr. Wyatt's Nutbourne; in 1862, at Battersea, by Mr. Phillips' Ellington; and in 1863, at Worcester, by Mr. Gulliver's Neville.]

A SECOND FOX.

"Well, gentlemen, what do you say? have we had enough, or shall we try for another? I am at your service, you know."

"Try for another," answers the honourable Mr. Hastie, who has gone a good one already, and would like to do it again—with "a second horse" to do it on.

"Had enough, I think," murmurs good man Yeomans, who is rather expecting the butcher to look at the bull-calf, and would like to go home to meet him—if the hounds go home too.

"I am sure there is a fox in ' the Firs,' " suggests the gallant Captain Closeshave, R.N., who has been distributing a bottle of " very curious" sherry with a most definite regard to such as have the honour of his acquaintance. They have managed to kill at the back of the Captain's house, and to bolt him subsequently; and the worthy host being no foxhunter himself, thinks if he can get rid of the gentleman in " the Firs" by the same coup, there may be some future saving of the " very curious" in question.

The Firs, " standing on a gentle eminence," as the auctioneers have it, look invitingly handy; the day is certainly not half gone, and old Closeshave stops with the gate in his hand, ready to show the way—

" Well, gentlemen, as you please, you know," repeats the Master, with the quiet, good-tempered smile of one who feels his hounds have already done their duty. "As you please. There can be no harm, at any rate, in just drawing these firs the Captain seems so certain about."

The honourable is "quite sure there can't." Even Muster Yeomans agrees "we may as well draw 'em now we are here"; and so, with an echo of his master's smile, Will gives the Captain a nod, and on we go for "the Firs."

"They are going to find a second fox," says Prudence, "and my nag has had quite his fair allowance with the first, and so I'll wish you good afternoon."

"But perhaps they *won't* find him," returns some more accommodating spirit than most men have under their waistcoats. "Old Closeshave is a jolly old humbug, everybody knows; and he is only too anxious to get us away from his sherry—and I dare say there is no fox there. Besides, the hounds' way home is my way, and society to a good fellow isn't exactly a thing to be thrown away—and, anyhow, the top of that hill isn't so much out—"

"—Oh, if you come to that," interrupts Prudence, a little roughly, "I ain't going to make a bother about it; let's go home with the hounds, or away with the hounds, as it happens. *I* don't care, if the mare don't."

"Well, the mare doesn't seem near so much out of sorts as you do, my friend; and so we *will* go. Here, give us a light, Squire; and let us enjoy this view at the top, if we can't get a view of the Captain's fox."

But Will is ready to do that for us, too, if it is to be done; so—"*Loo* in there, my lads. *Eu!* at him again, Conqueror, my man. *Eu!* push him up there. Get on —get on to him again, my merry ones!"

It is a fine exhilarating scene, at any time—the drawing for a fox in a good country; but it scarcely looks so well the second time of asking, particularly if you have had anything like a run with the first. The half-hour allowed between the heats has just been enough to stiffen the nags, and partially dry the dirt on them and the men's clothes. The very hounds don't draw with that dash that marked their first " charge" in the morning, but " *hoik-on*" far more methodically and soberly. Everybody, in fact, now it has come to the point, appears to think they might just as well have left the captain and his fox and his " very curious" for another day. Still he may not be here, after all, despite the swagger with which our adviser picks his way up the ride.

* * * * *

The Firs are half drawn, and not a hound yet shows a symptom of improving upon that somewhat indifferent air with which he entered them. Even Will's cheer becomes more cheery and confident, as he begins to think his day's work over, and that we shall go quietly home yet, when—*hark there!*—a challenge deep and strong. " Have at him, Conqueror, my man! Hark to Conqueror, hark!"—and there are twenty ready to back him. There is not much lying in the Firs at any time, and little enough now : he can't stop here long, that's certain.

" Hoik on! hoik on to him there," urges a whip, with just a cautionary crack to the tail hounds.

" *Tally ho!*" sings out the Captain, as a fresh, full-brushed, determined-looking fellow crosses the ride above him.

" Away! Gone away!" is heard from the upper end of the cover, hardly a moment afterwards ; and *away* he is, and no mistake!

* * * * *

" I thought there was no fox to be found here," says

Prudence, as you dig your heels into Margery's sides; "but then they may not be able to keep to him, or he'll be headed, perhaps; and as you only came up here for company, you may as well go on with them, now you have begun again."

Prudence suggests all this with something of a sneer, as "Who is right now?" But there is no time to parley with her, for the Captain's friend is threading a line of plantations, with every hound on to him. Their courage is fairly roused again by this; but Margery scarcely warms up so quickly, and it is all we can do to keep on terms with him.

"D'ye think the mare pulls as hard as she did?" asks Prudence in that very disagreeable tone she is occasionally in the habit of using.

But we haven't either patience or leisure to attend her just now, for Margery comes all but on her head at a bit of a drop, which Mr. Hastie flew like a swallow, and old Yeomans dropped into like a duck.

*   *   *   *   *

The Captain's fox turned out, in the especial vernacular of that distinguished service, "a regular clipper." He is known as such still in the three several counties he touched on. It is not my intention to follow him through the whole of "this splendid day's sport"—as they called it in the county paper—for I candidly confess that I did not see it—at least, not right out, from end to end. I went, however, as far and as well as I could, and I must do Margery the justice to add that she seconded me most nobly. Unfortunately, the further we went, on a proportionately worse understanding did I get with Prudence. It looked, indeed, very like coming to an open rupture, until Margery, herself in a great measure the cause of it, ended the dispute at an awkwardish stile, which she got over, a leg at a time—treating me to a terrible cropper on the other side.

This was the last I saw of it; in which long, lingering gaze the tail of Bob Hastie's grey in full flirt occupied a prominent position. I believe he was the last man left with them. But even he can give no authentic finish to the history of our second fox. He was viewed by a keeper, long after the grey cut it, just on the edge of "the great woods," with one hound coursing him, and a few more couple toiling on. If there *was* a who-whoop, it was Conqueror gave it him.

*　　*　　*　　*　　*

It was latish before I reached home, for Margery did not travel "express," and of course we had been running right away from home. Second foxes always do. When I did get back, the greeting was not a very warm one. It is astonishing how at times my wife and that Prudence agree in their tones, and the way of putting their questions.

"Why, good gracious, Mr. Softun, where *have* you been all this time?"

"Been hunting, my dear, of course; where do you think I have been?"

"Been hunting! Why, as I was coming through the village, not a quarter past two, I met young Mr. Choarist, the curate, coming back, sir. He told me the hunt was over early, and that you would be home before I should."

"Yes, my love, very true. But Choarist left after the first fox."

"The first! Why you don't mean to say any of you went after another? A set of hard-hearted wretches! I think you might have been satisfied with one."

"I think we *might*, my love."

A DESPERATE MAN.

They had a very pretty thing that morning—a quick find, with half-an-hour hard and fast tacked on to it—then a little slow hunting, and at him again for twenty minutes more, "heads up and sterns down," as the saying is, wound up with a very handsome kill in the open. Everybody allowed it was a pretty thing, except "the Major," who having gone rather better than best, put it down at once as "an almighty run and nothing else, sir."

The Major was altogether a model man—an officer and a gentleman—a gentleman and a sportsman—a couple of combinations that, whatever anybody may say to the contrary, we hold to contain no little amount of useful and enviable accomplishment. The Major was a handsome man, too, and a "gallant" Major, moreover, without any humbugacious, or *pro formâ* use of the term ; so that, when he sent up his name to the Squire, to say that he had called for a dinner—boots, spurs, and all—if the ladies would allow him, the said ladies gave three small cheers, as a free pardon and hearty welcome to the unexpected arrival who was showing himself in.

"It was a most almighty run, sir, said the Major again, as he took the first glass of the second bottle.

The Squire was in a bit of a fix, for he had got the gout, and couldn't ride or drink either; so there he sat, hearing how the Major had done one and seeing how he did do the other. Our honourable friend, if anything, too, was just a trifle egotistical in his history. Like Christopher North's, his recreations were nothing but what self did or self thought. *I* took a pull at the grey mare here; and the grey mare hopped over it there; and *I* and the grey mare were going just like oil—"

"Well but, Major, how did my boy go?"

The Major opened his eyes and filled his glass—said nothing, and expressed, in very pretty pantomime, that he knew as much.

The governor, however, pressed hard for the facts; the old man must live again in the young one; and, perhaps, after all, Georgy's horse may have eclipsed the grey mare, though the Major be loth to own it. "Come, tell us how he did go?"

How could the Major tell about the going of one who didn't go at all?

Patience and the gout are seldom very intimate; and the Major's mystery anything but added to his host's ease. "D—n it! out with it. What's wrong? What really was the case?"

"Well then, old gentleman, it was a case of funk. King Pippin pulled round at Exton-brook."

"What! the old horse refuse it? Never!"

"No—not the old horse exactly, but the young jockey. A case of funk, sir. Master Georgy must take a little more wine before he'll take water."

And the Major helped himself again, with the air and look of a man who never refused one or the other—in their proper places.

To an old "shelved" sportsman, about the greatest pleasure is to see his son playing a good part in those pursuits at which he himself was once so famous. However good the school reports, or however high the college honours, it is yet a sad disappointment to find the boy has lost all taste for horses and hounds. Our old friend, *in præsenti*, felt all this. Master Georgy was clever enough—with a head quite equal to all the trials the professsors had put him through; still the sire had hoped there was some heart left for the old home and old sports.

"Confound it, Major," he said, at length, with a deep sigh, "all this hurts me very much."

"Well, there's one comfort: you may take your oath it will never hurt him." And, with that, the Major agreed to finish off with the sherry; and went back to—"I and the grey mare."

There is only one excuse for a lad of eighteen not doing or daring to do, anything, and that is that he doesn't know what he's doing at all. The young Squire had this excuse. While he was pointing King Pippin at Extonbrook, he felt he was going right away, with a rightaway fox, from Exton vicarage; to which little paradise he had, on his own nomination, been appointed ambassador extraordinary, on this special purpose—to call, after the run was finished, and bring Miss Merton, willy nilly, over to dinner, and to stay a day or two at the manor house. Now, Nimrod and all the great writers assure you there is always a wonderful sympathy between the horse and his rider, and that the former can tell pretty clearly what the latter is up to. King Pippin felt it on this occasion. Instead of being rammed and crammed at the water, he found he was put at it "nohow," and so very politely "turned again," and off they went to the vicarage to lunch; the Reverend's man then riding him quietly home, and the young master, in due time, driving up with Miss Emmy.

Would any fierce neck-and-neck set-to with the Major and his grey mare compare, for one moment, with such a *tete-à-tete*?

We undertake to answer, for any young gentleman from eighteen to eight-and-twenty—"Unquestionably not; there is a profanity in putting it."

"Faint heart never won fair lady" is, after all, about one of the truest things that was ever said; for fair lady, however faint-hearted herself, can never forgive the whisper of such a crime in her champion. Poor Georgy who had been encoring "O, Summer Night!" participating in polkas, and getting as happy as could be, was a miserable sinner the moment "the gentlemen" came upstairs. The old Squire grumbled it out all at once, and tried to sneer at his son and heir the whole evening afterwards; while the tell-tale Major looked on for half-an-hour, and then "cut" most ignominiously, really sorry for the mischief he had occasioned. As for meek, gentle Miss Emmy, instead of comfort and consolation for the condemned one, she became amongst the most contemptuous and resolved of the ladies of the jury. "To make her the excuse for his cowardice, indeed! Why, if he had possessed anything like a spirit, he would have just ridden old Pippin over five or six of the most impracticable parts of the brook, and *then* turned away from the hounds, after having proved to all the majors and minors out how he could eclipse them, *if*."—She didn't say exactly this, but she looked it, which was worse, for there was no answering such a look; and so the rejected bowed himself off to bed, to tumble and toss and think over the strength of woman's love, and the pure, unalloyed pleasures of the chase.

* * * * *

"King Pippin is at the door, sir."

"What!" said the old gentleman, looking up from his breakfast with an air of well-assumed surprise, and the sneer "*continued*," as the magazine men say. "What! a horse that did such a terrible hard day's work on the Wednesday, to come again on the Friday?"

Sister Mary and Miss Merton "giggled"—the most horrible thing any young woman can do.

We fancy a hunter never shows to better advantage than when your man is walking him quietly up and down before the hall-door, ready for "Master," who is going to ride him himself to a handy fixture. Look at the brown horse now, how his coat shines, and the condition tells through it! What an air of coolness, resolution, and "up to his business" there is in that long careless walk! How the well-made saddle and broad rein, single snaffle too, set him off! Isn't there a proud pleasure and a good performance foretold in the very look of him? If we were a horse, that's just the time and place we would choose to have our portrait taken; or, if we were a horsepainter, that's just the time and place we would take it at.

It is a happy time altogether, that, to the man "who loves as he rides away"—when "the Missis" brings the youngest pet out to the door to "bye-bye" Papa; or, in case of uncoupled yet, when the blue eyes come to the drawing-room window, to smile you another " good-luck " as you look round for it.

Master Georgy didn't look round for what he wouldn't get, but went off with as little *éclat* as a bottle of bad soda-water.

"Hang the Major—the hounds—the hunting! Hang the little vixen, who"—no, stop. By the God of War!

he'll ride to-day, if there is anything to ride at, or, better still, any body to ride over.

"And so he did, like a man, or "like a madman," as the Major said, who settled it as temporary insanity at the second fence, where the young-un knocked himself and his horse through the unjumpable park-paling, and floored some hundred yards of my lord's boundary-line in so doing. This, moreover, instead of bringing on "the case of funk," as the Major, in very charity, hoped it might, only had the effect of getting his blood up the more; and straightway his majesty was sent, fearfully fast, at a double post and rail, which he took in a most wonderful "fly;" though, as "a matter of business," it ought to have been done at twice. They tell you, no man can count on a run when he wants one, or expect two good ones two days in succession. There is no rule, though, without an exception; and this promised to beat the Major's "most almighty" one all to fits. The Major himself, even, may be beat as well; but, fortunately, is still within sight as they come to the willows once more. Fortune be thanked! it's as wide as the Hellespont; and one man—the only man handy—has turned away from it already. Not so King Pippin, who is driven straight on by a nerve and a heart as hard as iron. Go he *must*—but not over; with a fearful crash he chests the opposite bank, while his unhappy pilot is flung, head over heels, far on to the meadow.

"By G—d! the boy's broke his neck," exclaimed the Major, pulling up short.

"He's broke his horse's back—the young devil"—said a whipper-in, who took a calmer and clearer view of the case.

It was a case for the kennels, instead of "the case of

funk," after all, with of course, as there always is, a lady in the case, at the bottom of it. Poor Pippin! may thy manes rest easy, and may thy fate forewarn all who would sacrifice to Venus what belongs to Diana!

How Georgy went home in a post-chaise, and his arm went home in a sling; how he was pardoned and reinstated; how he was nursed, watched, and petted; and how, when he did get about again, both the Vicar and the Squire agreed (with a " hereafter " smile though) that they were " really too young," hardly enters into this history. Enough be it to add that we'll give odds as to the Squire being a grandfather, and little Emmy a happy mother, long before the Major can again talk of pounding the " young-un" at Exton-brook.

THE LOVE BIRD.

"Rara avis in terris."

"Oh, Willie dear, before you go, I want a favour."

"Well, what is it *now?*" said Willie, in a gruff good-tempered sort of way, as if he was rather used to hearing of these 'favours.' Willie was an *officier de Dragons*, six foot three, with a great yellow, well-twisted moustache, and looking altogether just what he was—"a swell" *and* a gentleman.

"What is it, now?" asked Willie.

"Oh, please, then, don't be angry, but I've heard so much about them — and before you leave town, I should like it so much — you can get them in town, I know; and I only want one, just *one* — you know."

"No, but I *don't* know, you know. Come out with it, Polly—what is it?"

"Well, then—here, *whisper*—I want a Cochin China, please, sir."

Willie's weakness was a little, round-figured, light-haired, laughter-loving beauty, whose great point was to go with the fashion just as far as she could go. Charles Kean, the Crystal Palace Concerts, and the Cochin Chinas, all came in for a turn sooner or later—and Willie, glad, perhaps, to get out so cheap, swore "by Jove! she should have the best chicken in London."

Willie went on to his club, where he dropped at once on the man who knows everything, from what Lord Palmerston *is* going to do, down to what will really be John Scott's nag for the Leger. There are one or two kept at most of the clubs in town, little or great.

"Ah, I say, Smith, how are you? I want to buy a — a — a — Cochin China—Can you tell me where I can get him?"

"Of course I can, my dear fellow," says Smith, delighted; "The Corner for horses, you know."

"Ah—yes."

"Gunter for ices."

"Ah!"

"And Bailey for chickens."

"Oh—ah! thank'ee." Where is he to be found?"

"Close by here—Mount-street; your cab will take you there in two minutes."

And 'to Mount-street Willie went, where he repeated his wants to Mr. Bailey in propriâ personâ.

"Certainly, sir; will you walk this way, and allow me to show you some of my stock?"

"Well, no thank'ee! I don't know much about them myself; I'd rather leave it to you; but I want a good one, you know—one of the best, you know."

"Yes, sir, certainly."

"And send it to Thingammy Cottages, Alpha Road,

will you? and I'll settle with you when I come back to town."

* * * * *

"If you please, ma'am, the man has brought the fowl — *such* a big one! and please, where shall I put it?"

"Where shall you put it?—why where you always do, you silly girl—in one of your pantries, of course."

"But it's *alive*, ma'am."

"Dear me, how stupid of the people! but is'nt the gardener here to-day?—Well, get him to kill it, for I shall want it for dinner to-morrow, you know, as Miss Montmorency is coming, and I should like to give her a treat."

"Yes, ma'am."

* * * * *

When Willie got back to town again, the day after the dinner, matters evidently were not quite "to rights." Polly was half sulky—"he had disappointed her—had'nt done as he promised."

"But how?"

"Why, that horrid Cochin China—such a skinny, lanky, stringy thing, they could'nt eat a bit of it."

"Why, hang the fellow!" said Willie. "I ordered the best in London."

"Well, you only look at it then; I have kept it on purpose for you to see."

And Willie, on inspection, was fain to confess that he *was* "a leggy beggar, and a good deal overtrained;" and so went on to Mr. Bailey in a frame of mind accordingly.

"I say, you know, I ordered a Cochin China fowl from here the other day."

"Yes, sir—certainly."

"And, don't you know, I told you to send a *good one*, you know—one of the best sort."

"Yes, sir, I remember it perfectly; and the bird was sent as you wished to—"

"Ah—yes—but it *wasn't* a good one."

"Indeed, sir, I am sorry to hear that; I only know it was one of the best of my birds. Where may the fault be?"

"Well, he wasn't fat you know?"

"Perhaps not *fat*, sir," said Mr. Bailey, with a deprecatory smile; "in very fair condition, though, I'm sure. Anything more serious than that, sir, may I ask?"

"Yes, there was, he was tough sir, d—d tough!"

"*Tough!*" repeated Mr. Bailey, changing colour.

"TOUGH!" echoed the Guardsman; "they could hardly eat a bit of him. Why the deuce did'nt you send a good one, as I told you?"

"Sir," said Mr. Bailey, in a slow, emphatic tone of voice, "I am very sorry there should be any mistake; but I did send a good one—a great deal too good, I'm afraid, for your purpose. The bird I sent was one of the best bred in England. He was got by Patriarch, dam by Jerry—great grandam the Yellow Shanghai—great, great—

"Oh, d—n that!" interrupted the dragoon, "what's that got to do with it?"

"Just this, sir: six weeks ago I gave sixteen guineas for him at the hammer, and he is entered to you at *two-and-twenty*."

* * * * *

"It was rather an expensive feed you know," said Willie, as he commented over the story; "and by Jove! if the Missis goes on in this way, I should'nt be at all surprised if I have to give two or three thousand for a Short-horn, to get her a bit of beef for a Christmas dinner."

"The price of provisions has been on the rise for some time," said Smith—of the Club.

THE BELLES OF SWINDON.

(AFTER "THE BELLS OF SHANDON.")

With fond affection,
And recollection,
I often think of
    Those Swindon Belles,
Whose bright glance chains one,
Though not long detains one,
Or to lose the train's one
    Of the safest "sells."

Where'er I travel,
I can't unravel
What makes me cavil
    At all lines but thee?
'Tis thy Belles of Swindon
At whom I've grinned, on
A pleasant journey
    To thé West Countree.

I've seen Belles starring,
Full many a bar in,
When I enter dare in
    To your "Grand Hotels."
All with airs so striking,
Though to my liking
They sing but small to
    Those Swindon Belles.

For memory fleeting
O'er each kind greeting
We took at meeting,
  As we took our tea,
Makes the Belles of Swindon
The best to *tind* on
The traveller—speaking
  Hibernicè.

All fashion's mould in
I've seen dames strolling,
Or in carriage rolling
  By the Serpentine.
I've seen these dames, too,
As they went St. James through,
In silk and satin
  Look mighty fine.

But your look's more precious
Than any Duchess
Throws o'er the vulgar,
  Glancing haughtily;
Oh! you Belles of Swindon,
Who so kindly *tind* on
An old chap up from
  The West Countree.

There are Belles in masque go
To Jullien's last "go,"
When sainted Drury
  Weeps o'er their games;
In turn Cremorne, too,
I've seen them borne to,
On the pleasant waters
  Of the river Thames.

All these I grant 'em,
I do not want 'em,
For there's a quantum—
    Quite enough for me :
'Tis the Belles of Swindon
I've often grinned on,
As I rushed for soup, or
    I asked for tea.

THE FAVOURITE.

"I'LL take twenty to one in hundreds he wins," said the Commissioner, opening his book and his mouth once more.

" Done with you," said the public.

" And I'll take five to one he's first favourite before starting," continued the initiated.

" Done again," said the public.

But the many got tired first for all that, and the world —the sporting one, that is, of course—went home to bed with the firm conviction that " there was something up." The King of the Valley was going back visible, and the outsider was coming on quite as palpably: the King of the Valley, who won the Champagne in a canter, and out-paced the Colonel's flying filly over the T.Y.C. The King of the Valley, who had been backed all through the winter at under eight to one, and never been one hour amiss in his life, *was* giving way—and to what? To a nomination that nobody had ever heard, seen, or thought of before. It was all " flash," it *could* be nothing else— a mere bogy to frighten the considerate out of their calculations—a three days' wonder that must burst like a soap-bubble by Monday. And Monday came again, and the Commissioner came again, and took five to one again " he's first favourite before starting."

People began to take it up also—Manchester followed

suit, and brought the premier price down to four. The sporting sweepers went on with it, and bought him up right and left like safe shares from "capital" companies. The picture papers spared no expense, naturally, in gratifying such a taste, and exhibited correct portraits in all positions, from bird's-eye views obtained through quickset hedges, rugs, and quarter-cloths, or, as likely quite, from the mere force of imagination. The prophets went head and head with their brothers of the brush too, and showed in no time he had the finest shoulders and the stoutest blood of any horse in England. Moreover, the touts confirmed it all with curious cries of " curby hocks," "high blowing," "queer temper," "sore shins," and so on. *That* was enough, he'd got the ear of the whole world, and the voice of the majority; and so the commissioner bet his even hundred at once, just to settle the matter, that "he's first favourite before starting."

And so he was sure enough; and the Honourable Prior William Conqueror, as the happy owner, got more up in his stirrups, and quiet Mr. Make-believe, as the trainer, more mysterious than ever. The breeder, again, in the becoming pride of his heart, announced an "own brother," for sale for five thousand down, and four thousand more if *he* won the Derby. West-end exquisites went on their knees for "orders" to see him, and clever men with no acknowledged authorities or characters beyond their breeches pockets were equally urgent with orders to buy him. But the tact of Make-believe kept off the former as effectually as the faith of Prior William Conqueror did the latter. He had established an awkward precedent by presenting the horse of his stable to the lady of his heart, and so the grand event became one quite as much mixed up with love as money, honour—*subaudito*, as the guardian of both.

Time, tide, and Derby days, wait for few of us, and the unbelievers felt the crisis creeping on them with anything but agreeable sensations. The new wonder was heralded by the press as on his way to the scene of action, and a few words added on the commendable caution which characterised his transit. A lad inside to take care of the horse, and a policeman inside to take care of the lad. Mr. Make-believe on the box to take care of those under him; and the Honourable Prior as *avant courier* on his hack half a mile a-head, to order horses on, and shoot the first man dead that dared to ask a question. And then the choice of quarters again proved no chance thrown away in that item; none of your Spread Eagles public stables, or anything of that sort, where the opposition would have a hole ready bored, and a pipe of *aqua fortis* laid on before the crack had been in an hour. Nothing of that, but a nice lonely farm-house, all under our own command, and everything submitted to the most trying ordeal. Blacksmith searched and sworn to at the utmost value of his life before a shoe was moved or a plate fastened. Hay queried again and again, corn ensured as it came from home, and straw for litter ventured on at a handful a time. While, as for water—every soul with access to the premises drank regularly at every stable time an imperial pint to his own share, in witness of his sincerity; save and except only C. 99, who having as usual "unequalled opportunities" for perpetrating villanies himself in his official capacity of hindering other people, took a fair fourth of the bucket, and then passed it on with a clear conscience and small thirst to the noble "animal" (as some oracles *will* call a race-horse), whose superior capabilities had given rise to these attentions.

If unfortunately in these times we have no "Warren" open, to which by the bye, you had literally to "walk up," and see the lions, there is given us instead the yet more convenient paddock, and canter before the stand. And one rattled by, and then another—and another—and another, until at last with a warning "hie! hie! hie!" and a twelve or fifteen hundred guinea, useful sort of horse, in his clothes, just to clear the way, comes the crack himself—with a great sweeping stride, a coat shining forth like gilded gold, and a resolute long and strong pull at his jockey, that makes one half afraid he'll have honest Sim Simpleman over his head. Talk of being untried, or unknown, or trumped up for a purpose! look at him, only look at him now, as every eye of the tens of thousands is at this minute, and then offer your argument and odds against him. Odds, forsooth! half a point over eleven to eight, and you are nailed to your word like a bad shilling to a St. Giles' shop-board. "The gentlemen" are in the right box for once, and the ring will be done to a tinder. "A thousand even the favourite wins!" and his white jacket is up the hill and round the turn just where it should be—"the favourite! the favourite; the favourite in a canter!" And then there's a hustle, and cracking and closing up—and it's No. 3 instead of No. 1, after all—and the King of the Valley has won the Derby, and the favourite's broken down half a distance from home!

Of course it was just what might have been expected. "Men must have been mad, and nothing less, to back any 'animal' alive upon hearsay, to the tune they did: a horse, moreover, with scarcely a good point about him, while even the very fact of his coming of the 'Cat-gut' stock should have warned the world of the fate that awaited him. Was there ever one of them that could have obtained a warrant for tolerable soundness? In short, the favourite of this year affords us in all respects one of the finest specimens of humbug ever attempted." So said the prophets in their after-conclusions on "Sunday next," with a highness of tone and straightforwardness of condemnation that must have gone off uncommonly well, if they had not picked him out to a man, on the Sunday previous, as the only horse that could win.

* * * * *

"And so really, Mr. Holdfast, you don't think this death to the corn laws has done you much damage after all? You employ as many men, keep as much stock, use as many horses—by the way, what is this one coming towards us?—a bit of blood certainly."

"Aye! that it is, sir, and good blood they tell me."

"Why, however came you to take a fancy to one of that sort?"

"Rather he took a fancy to me—a gentleman sent him here for quiet, just before he was going to win the great race; and here he's been ever since. Cracked his leg, you see, almost, one might say, as he'd won more money than I likes to think of."

"Why, it *is* 'the favourite'—eh? Prior Conqueror's nag?"

"That's him, sir, ruined outright by it, and left his lamed racer here till his head got too big to get him out of the stable, and so in the end I took him for 'costs,' as the lawyers say. Stop a bit, Jack, and let the gen-

tleman look at him. Poor old fellow! he aint a bad
servant after all, for odd light jobs of this natur—is he
Jack?"

"Bad un, Zur! blowed if I don't think he's pretty nigh
as good as old Jolly now; ain't you, Bowler, my man.
Gee-Wut."

Bowler is the name, if you search for him in the Stud
Book.

THE LAST OF THE CHIFNEYS.

In an age now passed away the name of Chifney was as universally associated with the Turf as that of Kemble with the Stage. The one was a family of jockeys as the other was of actors. There was the Chifney rush, the Chifney bit, the hand of a Chifney, and the Chifney principle of riding a race. The art descended, as it so rarely does, as an heritage from the father to the son, and in forcible illustration of the Genius Genuine which they alike possessed. But it was not as jockeys only that the Chifney family were famous, for never, perhaps, was there a better judge of a race or a race-horse—no one with a keener or quicker appreciation of what an animal could do than the quiet, almost retiring brother, who stood by, while Sam was electrifying the world with one of his brilliant finishes, and living in every one's mouth as the great horseman of his time. Still, however, the public could go a little below the surface, and it was as " the Chifneys" that the brothers flourished in the very hey-day of their success, after standing so firmly by each other from their early dawn, when their father taught the one how to ride, and the other to train. And how well we remember them in their very zenith ! when the great treat of all that Midsummer holiday was a visit to Royal Ascot, where we were left on the Stand in charge of old

Ben Marshall, the painter, and never could there have been a better Mentor. Marshall, at that time, was the "Observator," or Turf correspondent of the *Sporting Magazine*, and got through his reporting just as he did his painting, in the laziest way possible, only too happy with some one to chat to. Time, alas! has rubbed many of his sharp telling remarks from the slate of our memory; but "that, young gentleman, is the famous bettor, Mr. Jem Bland; just behind him stands Gully; there's the General; and here "—sinking his voice to something really like a tone of respect, though no mortal had ever much less reverence about him—" and here comes William Chifney"—that spare, mild, gentlemanly-looking man, with so little "horsey" in his appearance, who is leaving the course as they clear it for the first race. There goes old Guildford, with that wondrous string-halt of his; and "Now my lad, look here!" That lengthy, tallish jockey, sitting so well home on the sweet little chesnut, is Sam Chifney himself, and his horse is their own Rowton, a Leger winner in his time, and which they are now backing for the Oatlands. And, despite the neat Saddler and the famous Lucetta, they win it too, and the Chifneys' horse becomes all the rage for the Cup. This was in 1832, but two years subsequent to Priam's Derby, when William trained, and Sam could only tell his namesake, Sam Day, how to ride, as Lord Cleveland would not give him up; while but three seasons previous, on this very course, Sam Chifney had won the Cup on their Zinganee, or, rather, Lord Chesterfield's when he started —against the finest field of old horses that ever were saddled—with Mameluke, Cadland, the Colonel, and Green Mantle amongst them. It was then that the Chifneys were omnipotent, with the finest houses in Newmarket, and the profuse style of living that caused their establishments to vie with those of the nobles of the land. No man ever had higher notions than poor William Chifney, for he was not a gentleman merely in manner or appearance; and we can well remember when going through the town on our way into Norfolk the following winter, how the very coach passengers talked of the Chifneys and their doings, as the smart mail phaeton rattled by. But even then the fortunes of their house were failing, though they knew it not, for they thought they had another Priam in Shillelagh; and they would have it so, as thousand after thousand was sent in to back him. In vain was it that the Jersey party shook their heads in almost mute astonishment and chagrin when they whispered to each other, as they left the heath, how "Plenipotentiary has beaten Glencoe!" The latter certainly did drop away in the great Epsom struggle, but with an honest jockey in poor Patrick Conolly, and such an owner as Mr. Batson, who refused any price for his colt, the Chifneys had no chance against Plenipo, perhaps the very best horse that ever ran. He failed, to be sure, as a stallion, but mainly, as we believe, from the injury inflicted on his naturally fine constitution from that fearful dose administered to him at Doncaster, when the horse reeled back to his stable in such an agony as no horse ever left a course before or since. There was no mistake about stopping him then. The Chifneys never fairly got over their beating with the Duke of Cleveland's horse, and although a year or two afterwards they had a good two-year-old in The Athenian, who was long a leading favourite for the Derby, he finished nowhere to Bay Middleton, and was out of the betting some time before the race. From this year William Chifney may be said to have fast sunk into the shade, a beaten man, and perhaps too proud a one to stoop again to conquer.

This is rather a recollection than a biography, but it may be as well to give an outline of William Chifney's eventful life. He was born, then, at Newmarket in 1784, and the senior by two or three years of his brother Samuel. His father was the first Sam Chifney, the great jockey of his time, and his mother was the daughter of Frank Smallman, once trainer to the Prince Regent, from whom he received a pension up to the time of his death. Surely there never was such a pedigree for a trainer or jockey, and the very maiden name of the senior Chifney's wife was suggestive of her sons' pursuits. She had in all, we believe, six children, Will, Sam, and four daughters; one of whom married Mr. Weatherby, of Newmarket, and another, the wife of Butler the trainer, was the mother of Frank and William Butler; while a third daughter, unmarried, died a year or two since. We gather from that remarkable work, "*Genius Genuine*, by Samuel Chifney, of Newmarket, published in 1804, and sold for the author at 232, Piccadilly, and nowhere else, price *five pounds!*"—we learn upon this good authority that Samuel and William Chifney were in the Prince's stable, where they "had but eight guineas a year wages, the same as the least boy in the stable, for which they rode exercise the same as other boys." But *Genius Genuine* is full of the author's troubles, and he complains of both his sons being turned "out of stable and house, from board," by Col. Leigh, the Prince's manager. What a wonderful book it is, with the quaint conceit of the very title carried out in every page! It was said some years since of the second Sam Chifney that he was "always funky when leading with a large field in his rear;" but we believe that his love of waiting was born and bred in him direct from his father, and if the family ever started a coat of arms, as possibly they did, their motto should have been that of the Roman General, *Cunctando*—free translation, " I'm a coming !" The father was always in hot water from disobeying or arguing over his orders. He would *not* make running, and how terse and telling is his description of one of those notorious races with Escape ! The Prince had wished rather than commanded him to make play, and " Skylark chose to make play, and I waited with Escape, and Escape won." This is a very epigram in its way, while in our refined times he would have " landed the dibs," or have done some dreadful thing or other of the same kind.

William Chifney naturally sided with his father, for the boys had been bred up to " use vengeance, so far as they were able, against insulting injuries ;" and thus " on the 31st of May, 1803, I was creditably informed Colonel Leigh had represented me to the Prince to be the worst fellow living. And, in those last October Meetings, as my son was standing by me on the exercise ground. Colonel Leigh, the Prince's equerry, rode, calling to Mr. Christopher Wilson, one of the stewards of the Jockey Club, to give Sam Chifney his stick to lick me with. * * * * Colonel Leigh was at me the same again on the race ground; and he knew I had been ill for two years, from losing the use of my limbs." What a picture this offers us of the manners of the age! although we have heard language almost as coarse upon Newmarket Heath within this year or so. And then " my son William, knowing of those and other insulting injurious usage of Colonel Leigh to me, himself, and his brother, and knowing, also, that I could get no redress from the Prince, nor by law, the boy licked Colonel Leigh." For this assault William Chifney suffered some months' imprisonment, but we must bear in mind the habits of the age, and the provocation he received. His father was, no doubt, old and enfeebled; for, if this was in 1803, he brought out his book in 1804, and died within the rules of the Fleet in December, 1806.

The son William, who, in addition to his father's instruction, had, of course, been a deal with his uncle Smallman, went on about Newmarket, until he had horses running there in his own name—Pendulum and a smartish filly, Romp, to begin with. Then came "the Chifneys" day with Lord Darlington, and their doings with Memnon and other high priced ones, though their success was not great. Again, there was Sam's engagement with Mr. Thornhill, with Will to help him, and Sam, Shoveller, and Sailor, all winners at Epsom in three years following; but, somehow or other, the jockey gets more the credit of these than his able adviser. Fickle fortune, however, gradually turned again against Mr. Thornhill, and by 1829, as we have already sketched, the Chifneys were doing more on their own account than for the Squire of Riddlesworth; they had Zinganee running, and the great Priam, for which William gave a thousand when a yearling, in work. Still, it was during this era of otherwise comparative calm in the fortunes of the Chifneys that William's fine judgment led to perhaps Sam's very finest bit of riding. In 1825 Will claimed Wings on the Wednesday at Epsom after her winning the Cup, and would only give her up to General Grosvenor on condition that his brother rode her, and not The Brownie, for the Oaks on the Friday. Wings won after a very close race, and the Brownie was nowhere. William Chifney, however, could ride himself if he so chose, and many is the hint he gave Frank Butler, who, with two such kinsmen to tutor him, certainly began with something in favour of his making a jockey. The elder uncle was a good man in many other respects—a capital shot, a crack walker, and a good man with hounds. But it was rather a melancholy sight of late years to meet him creeping about town, so far from the scenes and pastimes he loved so well.

William Chifney married a Miss Mary Clark, daughter of the well-known Mr. Vauxhall Clark, one of the first men who made betting a science, and did business by commission. By her he leaves two sons, Mr. William Chifney, who took to the study of the *Army List* as well as the *Calendar*, and who has held a commission in some branch of the Service. The other son, who attempted to follow the family profession, but soon outgrew the saddle, married a daughter of William Edwards, the well-known trainer to Lord Jersey—another race of jockeys. His uncle, Sam, left an only daughter, "Miss Sally," who became the wife of one of the Messrs. Isaacson, so that, as far as the Turf is concerned, we may be said to have seen "the last of the Chifneys."

THE BREEDING OF HUNTERS AND HACKS.

In a national point of view the good policy of calling more attention to this subject cannot for a moment be questioned, while the duty of doing so comes quite as legitimately within the scope of an agricultural association. All the rest of the world is even more inclined than ever to turn to us for their best horses, as for their best cattle or sheep. There is, in fact, no breed of animal that commands so ready a market as a good riding-horse; and yet, strange to say, there is no other branch of business so fortuitously supplied. Saving in Yorkshire, Lincolnshire, and parts of "the Shires," the breeding of horses is mere chance-work; and the very gentlemen of the district, when they are in want of a promising hunter or clever hack, have but too often to import him from elsewhere. The mere rumour, indeed, of a smartish four-year-old will bring Mr. Oldacre or Mr. Weston some two or three hundred miles specially to look at him; and dealers and their agents now attend our great summer shows almost as regularly as they do the autumn fairs, just for a glance over the hunting classes, already so attractive a feature in the proceedings.

And yet farmers will tell you that, as a rule, breeding "nags" does not pay; as, under the circumstances, it would be rather a curious thing if it did. As a rule, breeding such stock does not answer, because they are bred without any rule at all. In these days, if a tenant wishes to rear a good beast, he takes especial care to secure the services of a good bull, as with the same ambition he will bid up for a Cotswold shearling, or a Southdown ram. If moreover, he really means to succeed, he will be almost as scrupulous in selecting a dam, and, thus provided, he gives the principle he is testing a fair trial. But take the case of rearing a riding-horse, and how does the self-same man proceed? In nine times in ten "just anyhow." He puts anything he may happen to have with anything that may happen to come in the way. As often as not he scarcely looks at the horse he uses, but takes the word of some roving blacksmith, or broken-down coper who travels the country with an animal "best calculated to perpetuate the breed" of weeds and screws. Then the foal, when he does come, is cultivated much after the same fashion, or, that is, left pretty much to shift for himself. You will see him fighting for his own in the farmyard amongst a lot of store bullocks, as likely as not with a hip down, or a hole in his side from the thrust of a playful Hereford, and doing as well as he can on that grand specific, a due allowance of bean-straw. The result of this wonderful system is surely logical enough. At a year old the young nag is a half-starved, sulky-headed, big-bellied, narrow-framed thing, with most probably a blemish or an eyesore of some sort to complete his personal experience, and with a general expression and carriage as lively as that of Rosinante, or Dr. Syntax's Dapple. Very naturally the breeder of such a prodigy is more than anxious to sell him, but quite as naturally can find nobody willing to buy him; until, without heart, mouth, or action—under-bred, under-fed, and half-broke

THE BREEDING OF HUNTERS AND HACKS.

—the butcher gets him thrown in with his next half-score of beasts, or the village apothecary, on the spur of some hapless moment, is brought to believe that the colt may *suit* him! And thus it happens that breeding nags does not pay—with rather less outlay and attention devoted to such a business than one would bestow on a sitting of Cochin China eggs, or a litter of terrier puppies.

It may be argued fairly enough, that a farmer does not and cannot make the same wholesale business of breeding hunters and hacks as he does of producing cattle and sheep. Still anything that is worth doing at all is worth doing well, and this might be put yet more emphatically in a pecuniary point of view. There is scarcely an occupier of any position but who has always a goodish animal or two that he jogs round his farm, drives in his dog-cart, or, to say it out, rides with the hounds. Let these, or some of them in continual succession, be mares that from use, age, or accident, get beyond their work, and what then becomes of them? Their owner cannot sell them, and he will not kill them; so that almost as a matter of course and necessity he proceeds to breed from them. Let us not stay here to inquire whether they be just the sort for such a purpose; but let us, as the initiative, follow out the line of the Society, and show our friend that he should do, in contradistinction to that he too commonly has done. The great improver, then, of his species is the thorough-bred horse; and as a maxim, if you expect the produce of the half or even three parts bred mare to be worth rearing, you must put her to a sire who is as pure-bred as Eclipse himself. There may be occasional exceptions; but these are not to be trusted nor taken as precedents. A country mare crossed by a cocktail stallion may now and then throw a good hunter; but we shall generally find that such cocktails are as nearly thorough-bred as possible, and after all, it is safer to keep to the genuine article. When, certainly, we see a fine powerful three-parts bred horse, with plenty of substance and style about him, a good head, fine shoulders, clean hocks, and so forth, we feel willing enough to have a few more like him. But in this case we have a very forcible illustration of the fallacy of a proverb, for "like does *not* get like." Put the clever three-parts bred stallion to the equally clever three-parts bred mare, and can we do so with the assurance that they will reproduce anything as good as themselves? Most decidedly not. The great point, the very foundation of the personal excellence of the animal we have before us, centres on his being by a thorough-bred horse—a recommendation of which his own stock in turn would be as signally wanting. Nothing can be finer, as the experience of our recent Christmas shows went to prove, than the first cross between the Shorthorn bull and the Aberdeen cow; but what would be the result of crossing these crosses? Disappointment, uncertainty, and a thorough sacrifice of all purity of type, either from one breed or the other. A man who went on in this way for generations might eventually do something towards establishing a new variety of breed; but this, with such sorts as the Shorthorn and Polled already at our hand, would be scarcely worth the time and trouble; and I am not very sanguine of any enterprising individual inventing a better material for making a hunter than that he can get direct from the thorough-bred horse. What are the three great essentials of the modern hunter but speed, power, and courage? and where shall we get these but direct from the thorough-bred sire? There is nothing less warranted than the supposition that the English race-horse has deteriorated in strength or endurance. If you begin galloping him at a year and a-half old, to wear him out in running and "trying" before he is three years old, and his limbs set and his frame furnished, this is no proof of all he might have been, had his powers been husbanded like those of his ancestors, any of which, under like circumstances, he would have fairly distanced over a four-mile course. *Pace* is now the pass-word of the chase, and the best hunters in Leicestershire, either for fencing, weight-carrying, or stoutness, are, and long have been, purely thorough-bred. These are the horses that make money, and next to these the three-parts bred, by a thorough-bred stallion out of a well-bred mare.

But Jonas Webb, even at the acmé of his success, culled his rams, and many a Shorthorn that we never see has, like Brummel's neckcloths, been fastidiously put aside as "a failure." With the thorough-bred horse, however, it is not so: here, unfortunately, there are no failures. Those of the highest degree go to our famous turf studs to serve at their fifty or thirty guineas; others of almost equal excellence are eagerly bought up for the foreign market, while many of a similar stamp are put at prices varying from ten to twenty guineas. Such horses are all beyond the farmer's reach; but instead of looking for something in the next degree—and that, without the charge for mere fashion or high performance, might well answer the object—our breeder is too often content with the very worst of cast-offs. People who live by travelling stallions are not often men of much capital, and they go, as a consequence, more for a cheap horse than a good one. With a flaming card of all a great-grandsire has done, or what this very horse may have accomplished over a short course at a light weight, they associate an animal whose appearance alone should condemn him—narrow, weedy, and leggy, with scarcely a point in his favour for getting hunters, and very possibly full of all sorts of defects, natural and otherwise. The fee still is a small one, and so the mischief is done. A man pays 25 shillings where 5 guineas would have been a saving, and the thorough-bred horse gets a bad name, plainly and very palpably, if a customer would only make use of his eyes, from being unfairly represented. Considering the infinity of good or evil they are capable of producing, it is really a question whether horses should ever be allowed to travel without a licence, the more particularly when we see how few people take the trouble to judge for themselves. It is said that every Englishman is either a judge of a horse or thinks he is; but one can scarcely credit this, when we find such a number of weeds and cripples year after year earning incomes for their owners. Although nag-breeding may not pay, it is remarkable how many men still continue the unprofitable pursuit.

And now as to the remedy. The notion of encouraging farmers to breed a better sort of horse is by no means a novel one. The offer comes, in the first instance, by way of some recompence for the privilege of riding over their land, or to ensure their good-will for the Hunt. Hence, we have had Farmers' Plates and Hunters' Stakes, neither of which can be said to have thoroughly answered their object. The so-called hunter just "qualified" by showing at the covert-side a few times, and then went back to lead gallops for a Derby favourite, or to vary his performance in the field by winning a Royal Hundred. The Farmers' Purse, given by the gentlemen of the Hunt, has been often enough still further from its original intent. A sporting innkeeper or a hard-riding townsman would just "qualify," again, by taking the requisite number of acres of ground, and bargaining for a plater in due time previous to the race coming off. Then, by aid of a *quasi* gentleman-rider, who could sit still and finish, the "*bonâ fide* farmer" Boniface would pocket the purse, as the donors looked on year after year in glum disappointment, murmuring occasionally to each other that this was not exactly what they meant either! Perhaps, however, next to losing, the most unfortunate thing that could ever happen to a real tenant-farmer was to win one of these same Farmers' Plates. It has given more than one man of my acquaintance his first taste for the turf—another result as little intended by the founders of the prize. Still, let the members of the Hunt not yet altogether despair of what they may do in this way. Of late years the purse has taken a far more popular form, and in place of being contested as a plate on a race-course, it is now offered as a premium on a show-ground. To the growing interest and success of such a system I have already spoken; but we have scarcely yet got so far as the show-ground. Before we venture into public, we must see if we cannot set to work, and breed something fit to place before the judges. And here, too, the Hunt may help us. Let it be admitted that, in a free country like this, the licensing plan would hardly be practicable, and that any man may still "travel" any brute he chooses. Surely the fitting way to meet him will be to start a better horse in opposition. Let the Master and Managing Committee of the County Fox-hounds make it part of their business to see that the district is never without the command of a good sound, thorough-bred stallion "calculated to get hunters and hacks." Let such a horse, if necessary, be even the property of the Hunt, to stand at the kennel stables; and let him, moreover, serve farmers' mares at a certain moderate figure. Never, however, under any circumstances, let his favours be given gratis; for people are very apt to estimate that which they get for nothing at what they pay for it, and such a practice would only tend to make men more careless over a matter which they are only too indifferent about as it is. The principle I would here recommend has already been tried. It was only within the last year or two that I was staying with a friend on the borders of Shropshire, who was then looking out for another such stud-horse for the country, as they had just lost the one they had been using for some seasons. Baron Rothschild, who hunts the Vale of Aylesbury so handsomely, takes especial care that a thoroughbred one is ever within the graziers' reach at Mentmore; and the Duke of Beaufort has now always a stallion, which serves mares within the boundaries of Badminton, at a trifle over a merely nominal figure. I had the honour last autumn of awarding his Grace's premiums for the best yearlings by Kingstown, as well as for the best mare with a foal at her foot by the same horse, when the following suggestive incident occurred. The prize for the yearling went to a really blood-like filly, with fine free action to back her appearance. In the course of the morning I was accosted by her owner, a perfect stranger, who, after a word for the young one, added, "But you would not give the old mare a prize, sir." I did not know that I had ever had the opportunity of doing so, until my new acquaintance explained to me that she was in the brood mare class, acknowledging at the same time, "I know why she did not get it—she is not quite well-bred enough." And he was right. She was not well-bred enough, nor active enough to be either first or second of her order; and that wonderful nick with the thorough-bred horse had done it all for his filly — a fact which even a possibly partial owner saw as plainly as I did.

This brings me to another branch of my subject. Having secured the use of a good, promising horse, let us as early as possible go on to prove him. The four-year-old hunting class is the favourite one at our agricultural meetings; but I am not quite sure but that the yearling and two-year-old classes are not more advantageous in their effects to the breeders. In the first place, if a man has a tolerably good-looking foal, he may begin to keep him rather better than I fear many farmers are inclined to, if he thinks of exhibiting him as a yearling. Then, if he so chooses, this said exhibition may be something of a market. It is not every man who has the time or ability to " make" young horses; and there is always some risk in breaking, and so forth. A fair offer should consequently seldom be refused, especially if it comes at an early period in the colt's career; but this is a part of the business, again, that agriculturists are scarcely up in. If they have a good-looking young one, they are terribly apt to over-stay their time with him, and to keep him about home until he gets thoroughly blown on. A dealer has the opportunity of shifting a staymaker that no farmer can possibly command; and even further, this " making" of a hunter of a very necessity implies a deal of knocking about. A friend of my own once refused an offer of between two and three hundred guineas for a prize two-year-old from a neighbouring Master of Hounds, only to keep him on until from a series of mishaps the chesnut horse became almost unsaleable, and never afterwards worth a fifth of what was first bid for him! Others will become yet more enamoured with their own, and turn all their geese into ganders. Such a man will look at his colt until he finds him to be too good either to ride or to sell; and the coarse, fleshy, cocktail country stallion is the consequence. His owner's immediate influence in the neighbourhood is sure to get him some mares; and as he has never done a day's work in his life, he is possibly free from any very visible strain or blemish, a point that is equally certain to be made the most of. It is almost needless to say that the presence of such a stallion does infinite injury in a district; and if the weedy thoroughbred should not travel without a licence, it would be advisable to put down such an animal as this other one by Act of Parliament. Some gentlemen without any of the direct call of the M. F. H. will offer their friends the example of a proper model of their own free will. An enthusiast like Mr. Pishey Snaith, with a horse so well selected as old Theon — Captain Barlow, with Robinson replaced by Middlesex — and, I must add here, Captain Watson, with the Bishop of Romford's Cob, followed by Hungerford — must inculcate a most useful lesson in their several districts. Theon did wonders in this way about Boston; and, despite their vicinity to the capital of the turf, the farmers of Suffolk, until within a few years back, were quite willing to try and breed a hunter "anyhow," and from anything that came in their way. The improvement, thanks to the opportunity at Hasketon, I can say from personal observation in the county, is very remarkable; while the Devonians must know better than I can tell them how much they in turn owe to the Dorsley Stud Farm, which I had the pleasure of inspecting a year or two since. I have also seen the Beauties of Mamhead, where a similar principle is upheld; for although the illustrious Gemma di Vergy may be beyond our reach, I am glad to hear that since I was there Sir Lydston Newman has provided a second horse with such good stout blood in his veins as The Dupe.

It will be gathered that the point of this paper is a reliance on the use of the thorough-bred horse for improving our breed of hacks and hunters. Other crosses, with the *sine quâ non* of purity on one side, are of course available, such as putting the cart-stallion on to the blood-mare; but these extremes rarely meet or "nick," and are not to be recommended. A better plan would naturally be to associate the thorough-bred dam with the cocktail sire; but this, so far as the tenant-farmer is concerned, is practically impossible. It would require far too large an outlay to buy in the stamp of running mares fit to breed hunters from, and we must be content with what I believe, after all, to be the very best means for the purpose. No animal leaves a stronger *imprimatur* of himself than the racehorse; and though he may not be big and bulky, he will often throw back to more size and power. The cross put the other way is not common, neither can I remember any such striking examples of its success as, even if possible, to warrant its more general adoption. Nearly all our best steeplechase-horses, if not themselves quite thorough-bred, have claimed thorough-bred sires; and I may cite an example in this way that came personally under my own observation very early in life. My father had for many years in his stud a thorough-bred mare called Pintail, by Pioneer, that, just towards the close of her career, threw that famous steeplechase horse, The British Yeoman, by Count Porro. Her previous produce, however, had been anything but superior, and, as a chance for embuing them with a little more stoutness and substance, she was put one season to a good-looking three-parts-bred stallion that was travelling in the district, the result being unquestionably the veriest weed of the whole family. As for the Yeoman himself, light wiry horse as he was, nothing but his pure lineage could have carried him through dirt and under weight in the way it did.

We must, then, insist on " a thorough-bred stallion to get hunters and hacks" as the main principle to go on. Such an animal, as I have already intimated, need by no manner of means have been a famous racehorse—a fact that of itself would go to place him beyond our limit, at the same time that it is anything but an indispensable item in his qualifications. The chief things we have here to look for are true symmetry, good action, a staying pedigree, and freedom from hereditary taint; a deep frame, a round barrel, on a short wiry leg; a sensible rather than a "pretty" head, a well-laid shoulder, a good back, and plenty of bone. Never mind if his powerful quarters do droop a bit, so that they run down into big clean hocks and thighs; and do not care to dwell too much over an accidental blemish, or even a fired fore-leg, so that the leg itself is of the right shape and calibre. Above all, do not mistake mere beef for power; and in the thorough-bred horse, over all others, go for wire, muscle, and breeding, in preference to what may look like more substantial qualities. In this respect some of the authorities of the show-yard, who are called upon to decide over sheep, pigs, chaff-cutters, *and* hunter-stallions, still require a little tutoring. In the " what to avoid" we must guard against soft flashy strains of blood that are of no value beyond the T.Y.C., and hereditary infirmities of all kinds. Bad eyes, bad wind, bad hocks, and suspicious ring-bone-looking fetlocks are all very bad things in a stallion, the more especially if you can trace them. A horse may be blind from accident or ill-treatment, and one of our most eminent veterinarians has assured me that he did not think there were half-a-dozen stallions in England that were not roarers. The injudicious manner, however, in which many stud-horses are kept, what with high feeding, hot stabling, and little exercise, might account alike for diseases of the eye and the respiratory organs. Still beyond what you may deduce from actual appearances, it is always as well to look back a little into the genealogy of the thorough-bred horse. Some lines, for instance, are notorious for the noise they make in the world. Humphrey Clinker, the sire of the famous Melbourne, was a bad roarer, as was Melbourne himself, and as are many of his sons and grandsons. Another celebrated Newmarket horse was known to get all his stock with a tendency to ringbone; and weak hocks give way so soon as you try them. There are clearly-admitted exceptions: a stone-blind stallion will get animals remarkable for good eyes, and a thick-winded horse may not reproduce this in his progeny; but as a maxim, wind, eyes, and hocks should be three essentials of anything *sound* enough to breed from, be it either sire or dam. I would not so much declare for a big horse as a fair-sized one; and the saying of a good big horse being better than a good little one is not quite such a truism as it sounds to be. Fifteen two or fifteen three, with bone and substance, is big enough for anything; and when we come to bear in mind the sort of mares such a horse is to be put on, it is perhaps preferable to anything higher. For my own part, I go very much with the Cline theory, which says: "It has generally been supposed that the breed of animals is improved by the largest males. This opinion has done considerable mischief, and would have done more injury if it had not been counteracted by the desire of selecting animals of the best form and proportions, which are rarely to be met with in those of the largest size. Experience has proved that crossing has only succeeded in an eminent degree in those instances in which the females were larger in the usual proportion of females to males; and that it has generally failed where the males were disproportionately large. When the male is much larger than the female, the offspring is generally of an imperfect form." It must have been some such opinion as this which caused that rare sportsman, the late Sir Tatton Sykes, to breed from none but small or moderate-sized sires; and I believe that the cross of the Exmoor pony with the thorough-bred horse would be yet more successful were the latter only a little more proportionate to the size of the mares. It would be pleasant to hear that Lord Exeter had lent them his handsome little Midas for a season or two, when we might expect to see in the produce some of the most perfect hacks ever backed. Not the hideous, vulgar, heavy-shouldered, loaded neck Prince Regent kind of cob, but a little pattern of beauty and strength, with style, substance, and action really fit to carry a king. Such a hack as this would soon outplace even the Prickwillows and Phenomena, already going out of use for the saddle, now that men travel to meet hounds in first-class carriages, and the feats of Dick Turpin and "The Squire" are fast becoming mere matters of hearsay. Like the modern hunter, the modern hack must be well-bred, and we couple the two in the requirements of our stud-horse. If a country breeder wishes to ascertain for himself the description of riding-horse that is likely to make the most money, I would recommend him to stroll into Rotten Row, between one and two during the approaching season, where he will find here again how "blood will tell," and what Mr. Rice and Mr. Quartermaine have to go in search of.

Will the man who means to do better and give nag-breeding a fair trial be good enough to bear in mind that much of all I have said as to the sire applies equally to the dam? Let there be some shape and make, with health and action, and the same warranty as to wind, eyes, and hocks. With rarely any pedigree to fall back upon, appearance and soundness must be the chief recommendation of the farmer's mare; and even such a verdict based upon such conclusions must not be too hastily arrived at. Many a comparatively mean-looking one has before now thrown the best of stock, as that peerage of their order, the *Stud Book*, would assure us: mares that need carefully looking into before they are condemned or passed over. To give an illustration, however, direct to our purpose: about the grandest cocktails I ever saw were Mr. Foster's Combat, Challenger, and Niké, all capital runners at welter-weights, and all the children or grandchildren of, I am assured, as common-looking an animal as could be. The old mare had, no doubt, much within her "that passeth show," brought out as this was by the cross to the thorough-bred horse. In fact, if the dam be but clear of hereditary unsoundness, and with good action, I do not think we should be too scrupulous in asking the tenant to send nothing but the great fine slashing mares which they would, as half-bred, be scarcely justified in buying up. A friend in Devonshire has sent me a few lines on the way in which the "packhorse" answered to the superior cross, that I must give here: "The true packhorse is extinct, and has been ever since my horse recollection, that is, for about the last twenty years. The animals then going, in 1840, called 'pack,' were out of pack mares, but their sires had crosses of blood or Yorkshire. Old Gainsborough, the thorough-bred of household notoriety in Devonshire, one who flourished somewhere about 1830, is generally credited with *never having got a bad one*. I attribute this to his being the first cross with the true old pack mares; and I believe that any moderately good thorough-bred would have produced a similar result, could he have had a chance with the same sort of mares. The animals resulting from Gainsborough and these pack mares—and I have several in my mind's eye—were perfection in make, shape, and action, weight-carriers, everlasting, perhaps scarcely speedy enough for the present fashion of spurting across the grass countries, although safe to shine through a severe thing and be in at the finish. This Gainsborough generation of riding horses has also gone, and *no young Gainsborough cocktail stallion ever got a good horse*. It is a public misfortune that the line of the old packhorse has not been continued in a pure stock, both for his own excellent inherent qualities, and for the value of the first cross with the thorough-bred. The big half-bred mares of this cross put again to a good sound thorough-bred sire produced the animals to go the pace and carry the weight brilliantly in any country, and this is my pet process for a breeding line."

Of late years the West Country farmers appear to have been crossing and re-crossing out of all rhyme and reason, until they have nothing left but the horse of all-work, which, as was amusingly demonstrated at the Truro show, they hardly knew how to class, either as a riding-horse or as a common draught-horse. However, as my friend adds, "every Devon farmer, as a rule, breeds or tries to breed riding-stock, and, as a consequence, in some hole-and-corner holdings a stylish promising nag colt is often dropped upon where a stranger would think it about as likely to find an elephant."

So much for a fitting foundation. But let the thorough-bred stallion, under the countenance of the Hunt, be ever so well adapted for his purpose, and the mare really worthy of his caresses, the business of breeding is yet only in the beginning. Better bred stock require better treatment, and pay better for it. Half a horse's goodness, as it is said, goes in at his mouth; and it will be idle for farmers to attempt rearing riding-horses without they do them a deal better than, as a rule, they hitherto have done. A half-starved foal never forgets it; and from the day he is dropped he must be the object of some care and attention. Does the dam give a good supply of milk? Does the young thing look as if he was doing well? Let his feet be looked to, as he grows on; and, above all, let him be well kept, have a fair supply of corn, comfortable, sheltered quarters, and so forth. I am no advocate for over-coddling, nor would I wish to see the hunting-colt brought on as if his mission was to win the Derby; but liberal rations, kindly treatment, and gentle handling will all tell by the time he is first led into the show-ring, or delivered over to the breaker. I confess to having some dread of that same country breaker, with all his wonderful paraphernalia and apparently indispensable habit of hanging about public-houses, as a means of making young horses "handy." No man needs more watching; and, as I have just intimated, a vast deal may be done towards making the young one temperate before ever he reaches this trying stage in his career.

The horse is by nature a social animal; and, especially after weaning, two or three of the foals will do better in company, due care being taken that any one of them does not become too much of " the master-pig," and get all the good things for himself—to correct which they should be separated at feeding time. When together they will challenge each other to " strike out " a bit; whereas the solitary mopes about with but little incentive to try his paces, and is much like a boy brought up at his mother's apron-string, or a young foxhound that has lost his friends. I should hope by this that a duly qualified veterinary surgeon is within hail of most farmers, and I would leave it to this gentleman to throw his eye occasionally over the little stud, arrange the proper period for castration, and other such detail that will necessarily have to be adapted to time and place. On any such minutiæ of the matter it is not within my purpose here to enter, even if it would be profitable to do so. This paper rather professes to deal with the great principles of breeding riding-horses, and in seeing these carried out with a little more heart and judgment than they generally have been.

One word more for the veterinarian. Nothing can be more wholesome than the regulation which, after considerable discussion and division, the Council of the Royal Agricultural Society are still able to insist upon as part of their proceedings—viz., that every horse entered for exhibition shall be examined and passed by a duly-appointed veterinary surgeon previous to his facing the judges. It is true that the latter should and might be able to reject an unsound animal without such assistance; but their edict would not carry the same weight, especially with the disappointed owner of a disqualified horse, as the professional opinion of the College-man. It is scarcely fair, in fact, to place gentlemen who give their services to the Society in so invidious a position—one that often renders them liable to much gratuitous abuse. I would not, however, have the veterinary inspector of the meeting in any way interfere or intrude upon the judges when work. His duty is to see that none but sound horses before them, and there to limit his responsibility. ..etimes it will happen that the judge will associate the ...o offices in his own proper person; but as a rule it is better that the Society should appoint its own veterinary surgeon. Of course, such an examination should not be confined to the stallions, but extended to every class of horses in the entry. It is somewhat significant to reflect how resolutely this plan has been resisted in certain quarters, and by certain exhibitors, not merely at the meetings of the Royal Agricultural Society. I know at this moment of a country show of some repute where the presence of the veterinary-inspector has been for years successfully tabooed, until the number of unsound animals exhibited has justly come to create some alarm for the character of the breed. I am speaking here rather of cart-horses than riding stock, while I am glad to see that a leading member of the direction has put himself to reform this too-flattering fashion of making up a show, and that a preliminary veterinary examination is now embodied in the rules and regulations.

It is very clear that within the last few years the proper stimulus has been given for breeding a better description of "nag-horse," and I am sanguine of still-continued improvement in this way. I have seen most of the famous horse-shows, and had the pleasure of being

present at that grand meeting at Middlesborough, w[here]
the first hundred ever offered was won by Lord Ze[tland's]
celebrated Voltigeur; from the great success of [this]
occasion the national association was induced to inst[itute]
a similar premium. The Bath and West of En[gland]
Society is now following the same course, and [there is]
every prospect of this very agreeable feature i[n the]
business of the farm being more systematically deve[loped,]
with proportionate advantage to the breeder and [also]
to the country.

The Farmers' Club, London, Jan., 1863.

www.ingramcontent.com/pod-product-compliance
Lightning Source LLC
Chambersburg PA
CBHW020913230426
43666CB00008B/1432